ALL I SEE IS YOUR GLINTING

90 Days in the Pandemic

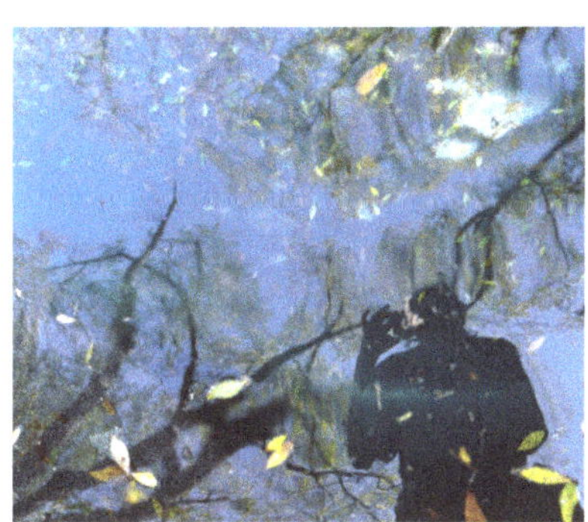

What people are saying about *All I See Is Your Glinting:*

Gianna Russo's dailies—haiku-like poems—mark the seasons of the plague. She deftly mines the shifting emotions, the fear, the fleeting beauty, the frustrations, and the sudden joys of each passing day. Jenny Carey's photographs tell their own story at the nexus of the manmade and natural worlds, her meanings often spelled out in the crinkled letters of fallen leaves. *All I See Is Your Glinting* is a pitch-perfect chronicle of our shared year of masks and menace, alongside the muted doings of daily life.

—Paul Wilborn, author of *Cigar City: Tales from a 1980s Creative Ghetto*

In this poignant and gentle book, poet Gianna Russo strikes out to cross the pandemic in a form that she has invented, the daily. Each day is an image, a number of words, and an attempt to contain fear and make sense of the wrenching fragility that had become viral and global. Paired with Jenny Carey's healing photographs, this innovative and luminous book goes straight for the heart.

—Janisse Ray, author of *Red Lanterns* and *A Cracker Childhood*

ALL I SEE IS YOUR GLINTING

90 Days in the Pandemic

poems by Gianna Russo
photographs by Jenny Carey

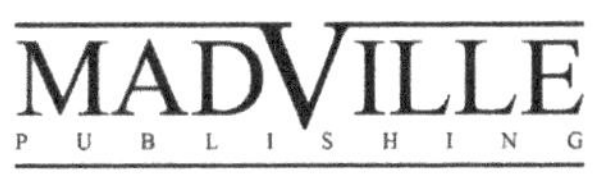

Lake Dallas, Texas

Printed in the United States of America

FIRST EDITION

Requests for permission to reprint material from this work should be sent to:

Permissions
Madville Publishing
P.O. Box 358
Lake Dallas, TX 75065

Author photograph of Gianna: Lou Russo
Author photograph of Jenny: Kimberly DeFalco
Cover photo: Jenny Carey

ISBN: 978-1-948692-99-1 hardback
ISBN: 978-1-956440-00-3 paperback
ISBN: 978-1-956440-01-0 ebook
Library of Congress Control Number: 2021946225

From the poet:

for Phyllis

From the photographer:

for the women who built me:
Jennie, Libby, Bertha, and Alice Carey

TABLE OF CONTENTS

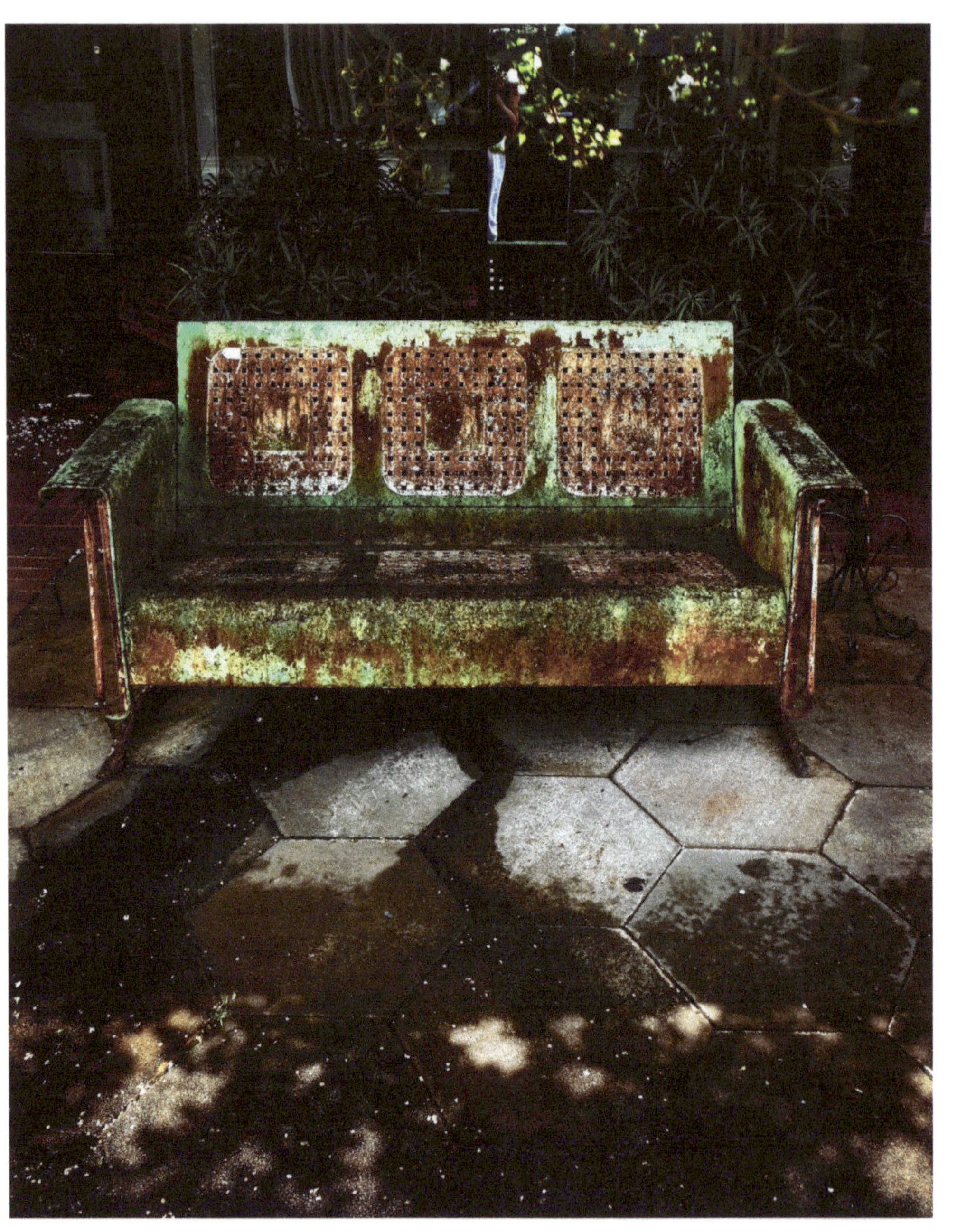

October 2020

Blue Ridge Mountains,
North Carolina

10/1

Leaves goldening.
But not
enough to
block the
wild boar
world.

10/2

How distant
it seems,
that night
toasting friendship
on a
glittering riverbank.

10/3

Dining out
was one
happiness. At
home, caution
sets the
table. Wine
trembles.

10/4

Venus, a pewter
lamp, dogs
us along
the mountaintop.
Virus and
death stalk
even here.

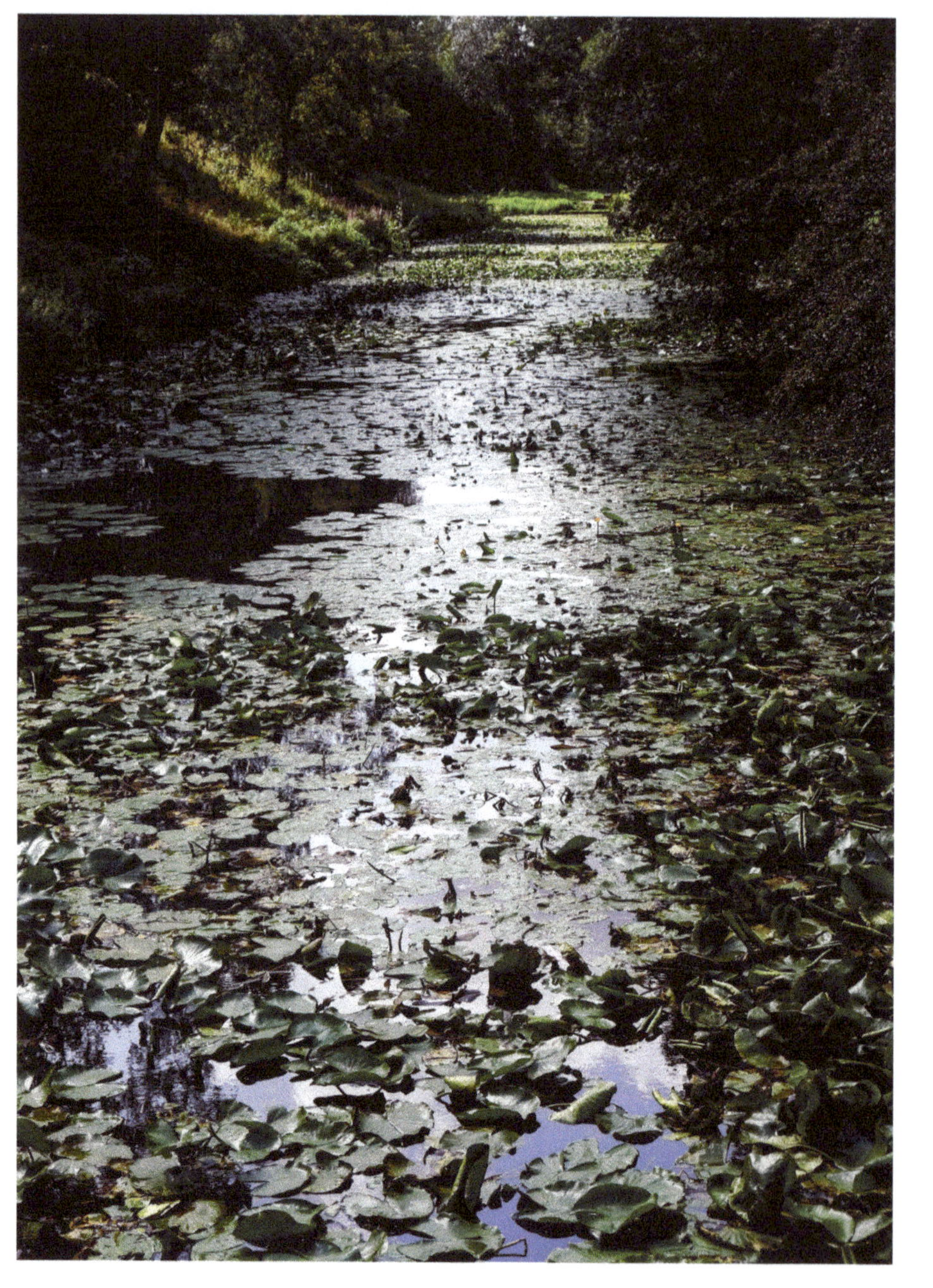

10/5

Staring into
clouds, we've
escaped for
a while.
Beech silhouettes
concede our
bravura's
clumsy
collapse.

10/6

Unfolding blue
cotton linens—
mildewed scent
amidst antique
roses. Feels
like we
haven't slept
in years.

10/7

Autumn afternoon,
mountain trail.
Black woman
emerges from
dappled light,
her solitary
happiness
spurning
the pale trees.

10/8

Baying hounds
and gunshot
reverberate through
the valley.
Hunting's prohibited.
Screech owl
trills the
law: broken,
ignored, thrown over.

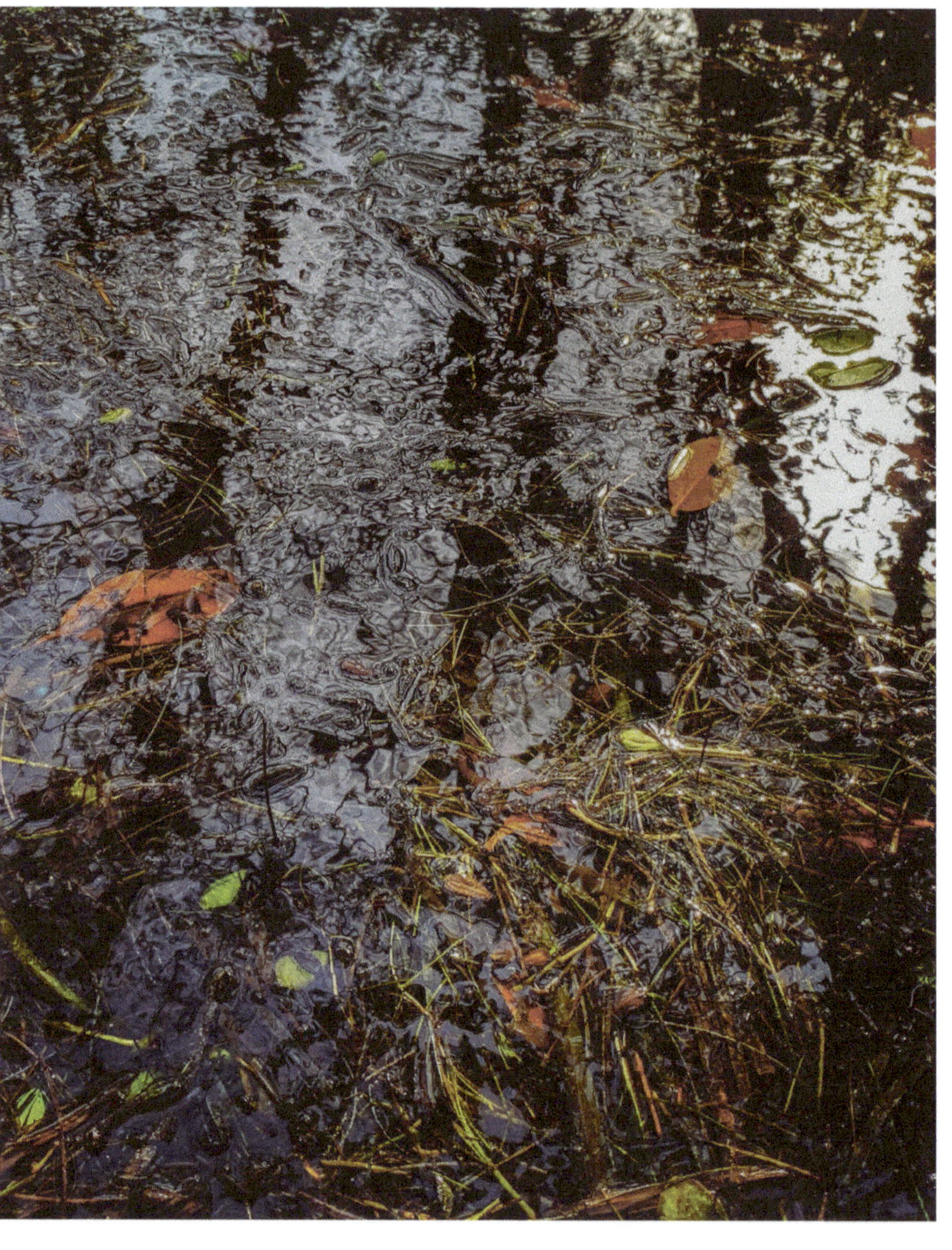

10/9

Buff-colored doe
blends into
road-bend, masked
in leaves,
an Escher
print. We
stare, awed
by realness,
her coal-dark
eyes.

10/10

Wild turkeys
step down
mountain steepness,
upright as
ministers. Their
combs disappear
last, fallen
dominoes. Elsewhere,
the news
plays out.

10/11

The world
below is
opaque, pure
cloud, as
white storms
overtake the
valley. Blanked
out, we
commiserate
with orphaned,
rain-rippled maples.

10/12

White, black,
brown mares
in a sepia
field.
Splotches of
Queen Anne's
lace, barbed
wire. Earth-scent
must be
the heaven
we have.

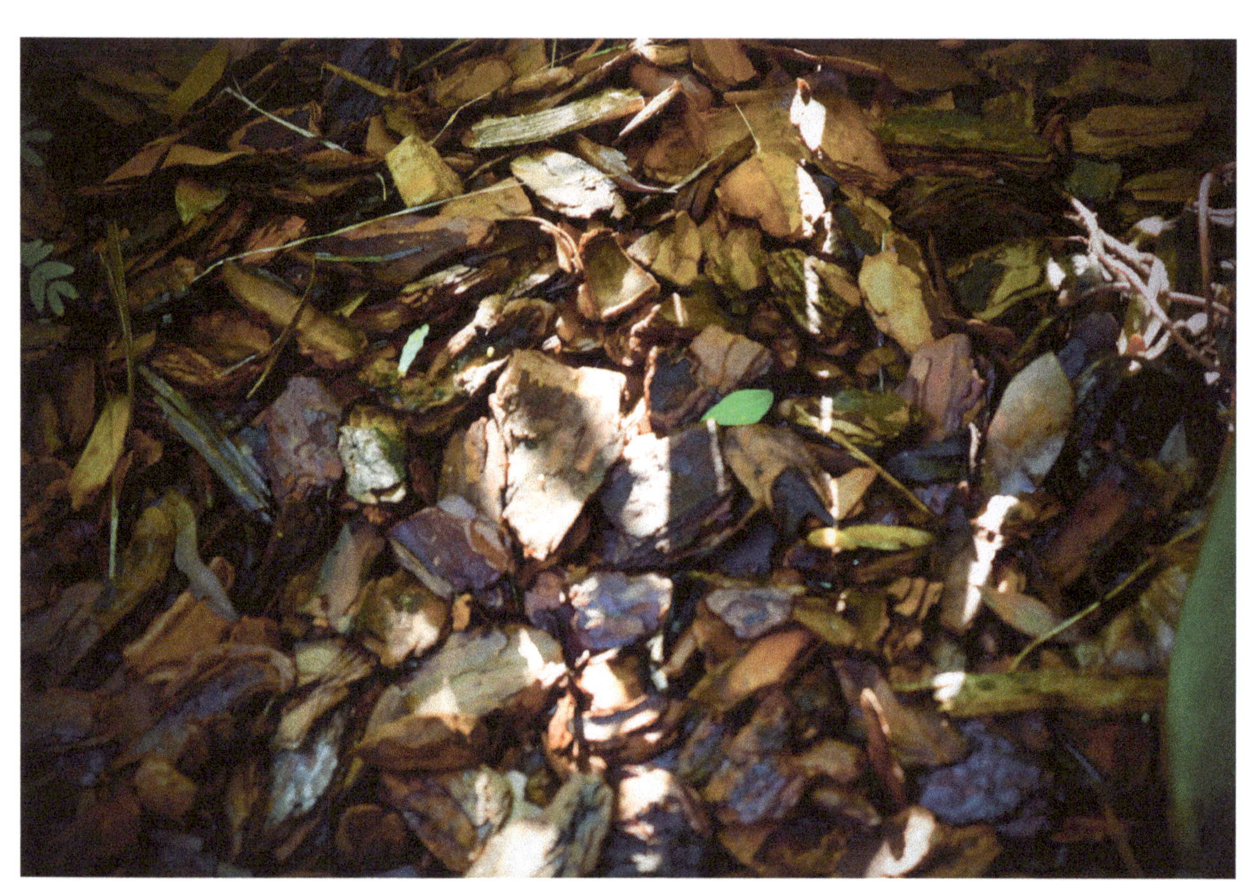

Tampa, Florida

10/13

His voice
a pitiful
tumble of
vowels, my
cat registers
his complaints
concerning our
week-long disappearance.
Poor bewildered
thing, wondering
where absence is.

10/14

Molting, eggless
neighborhood chickens
are coop-crazy,
gossipy, itchy.
October in
Florida twins
with scorching
August. Feral
roosters broadcast
warnings:
another day
of climate
change.

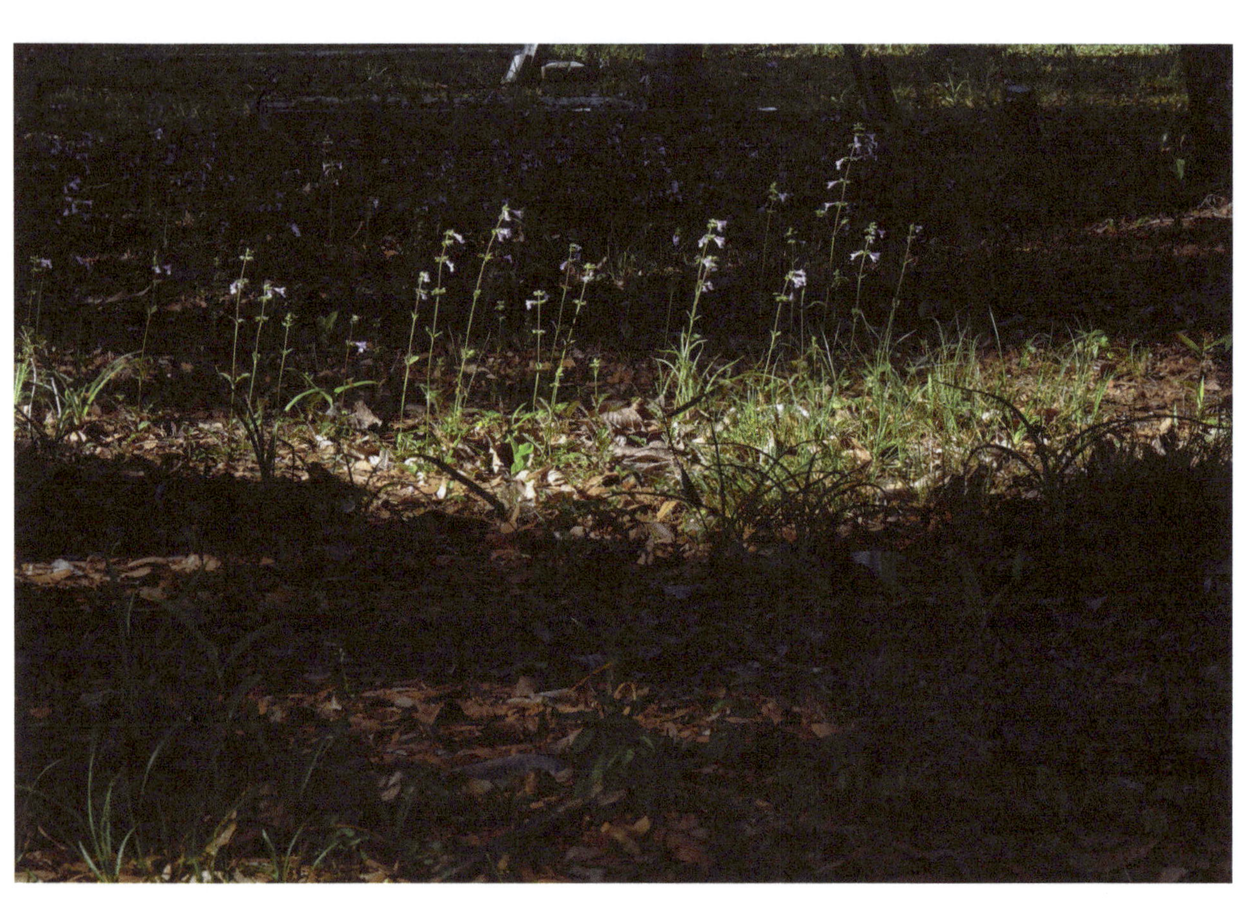

10/15

Carpet moth
in my
palm, holy
in its
stillness, fluted
wings V-ing
towards the
furred body
small as
a child's
thumb. Death's
sting right
here.

10/16

Instead of
hawk, copter.
Instead of
hoot owl,
squalling siren.
Not mountaintop,
but sea-level.
Fall . . . back
to summer.
Thursday morning
train whistle.
Inside it,
owl's voice.

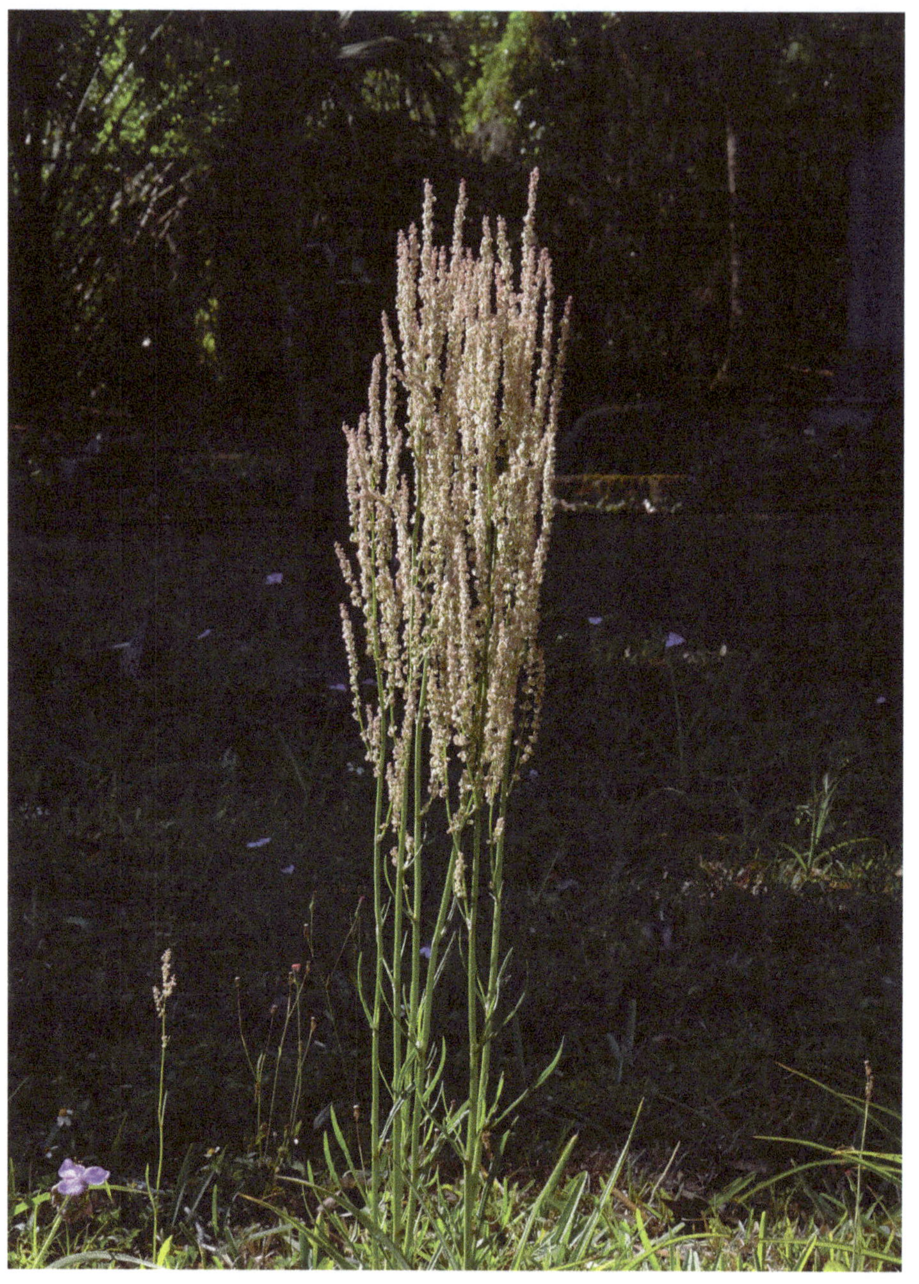

10/17

October yards
branded, cleaved
by political
signs, my
choice and
the other.
Meanwhile, the
antlered virus
stomps webfooted
over continents,
trampling us.
Gardenia bush
sags, bloom-starved,
scentless.

10/18

A coven
of black
hornets stings
my eye,
my face.
Yowling, I
stumble for
your help.
We whisper, *You.*
No, you.
Each vowing
not to outlive
the other.

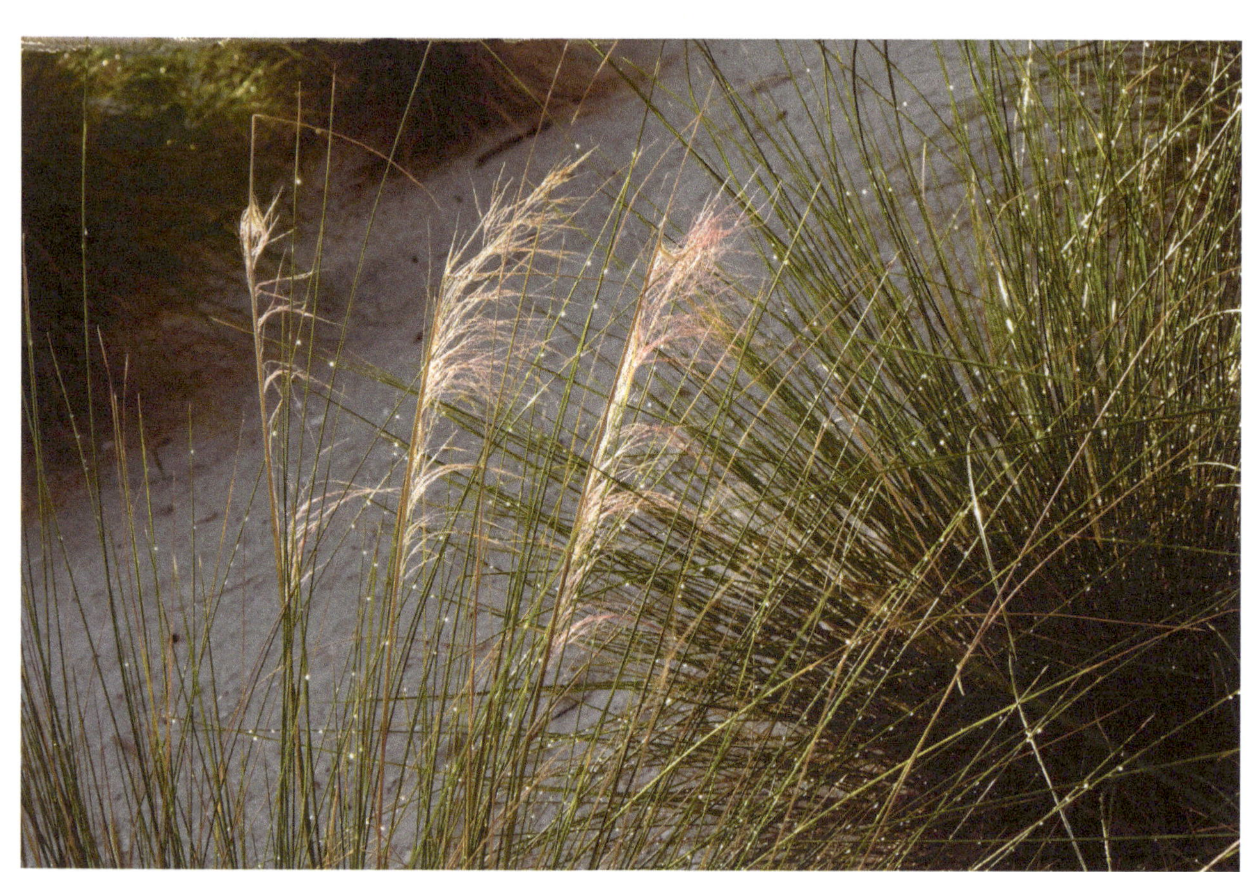

10/19

Busyness rushes
me from
screen to
screen, ring
to beep,
click to
clatter. How
quiet the
days must
have been
before our
interconnectedness.
I don't remember
them at all.

10/20

Early voting,
mail-in ballot
drop off
day, a
squall of
showers drenches
West Tampa.
Poll workers
are ready,
eager, smiling.
Lone white
man stomps
off huffing,
frowning,
without
a mask.

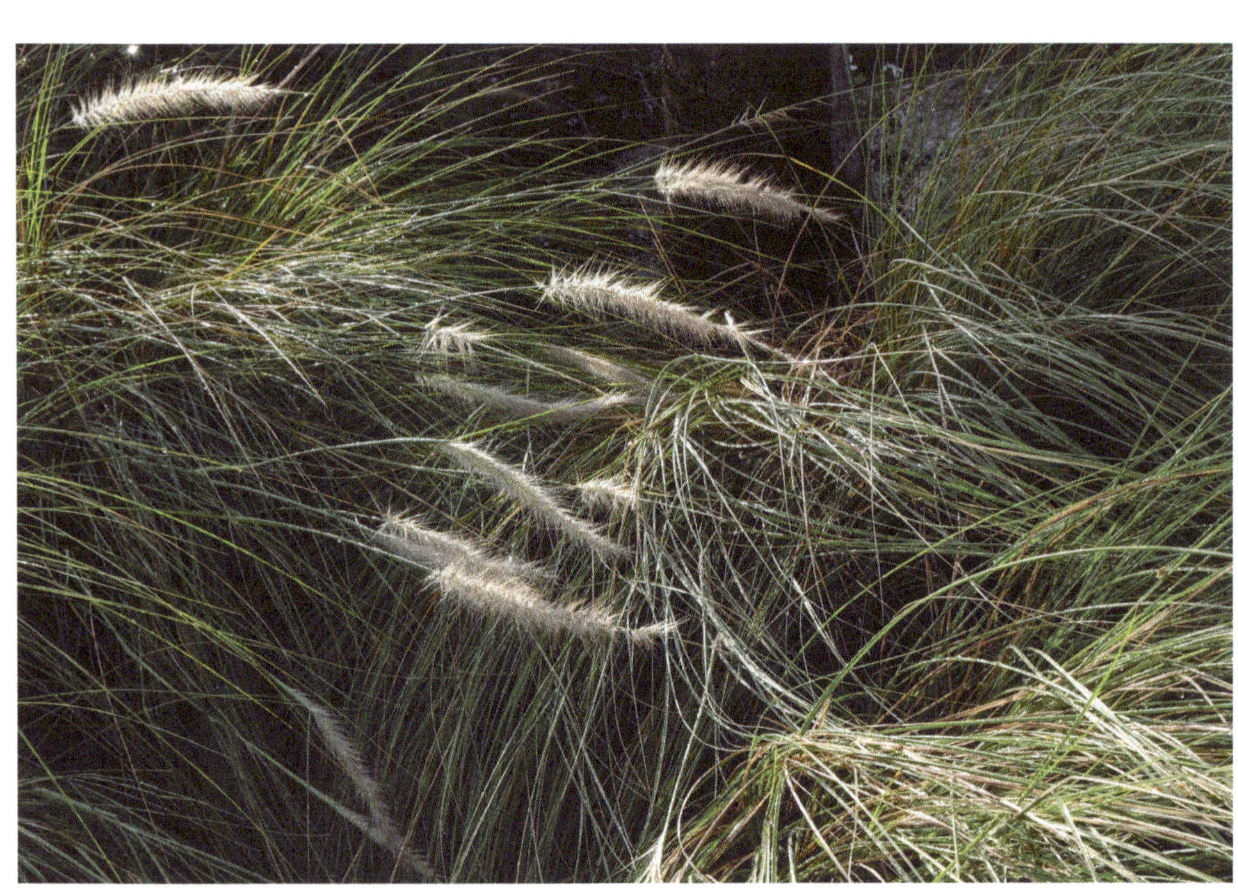

10/21

Chalk scribbles
on the
porch floor
remind me
how art
can enchant
us. The
world is
all pewter
coins, razors,
ashes. Flow
transforms all
that into
roses, broaches
of silvered
joy.

10/22

Blue jays,
finches, Carolina
wrens worry
all morning,
piping out
torrents of
warnings and
commands. It's
just me
moving blue
porterweed from
cloud to
sky, just
me sweating
in ragged
buttercup mansions.

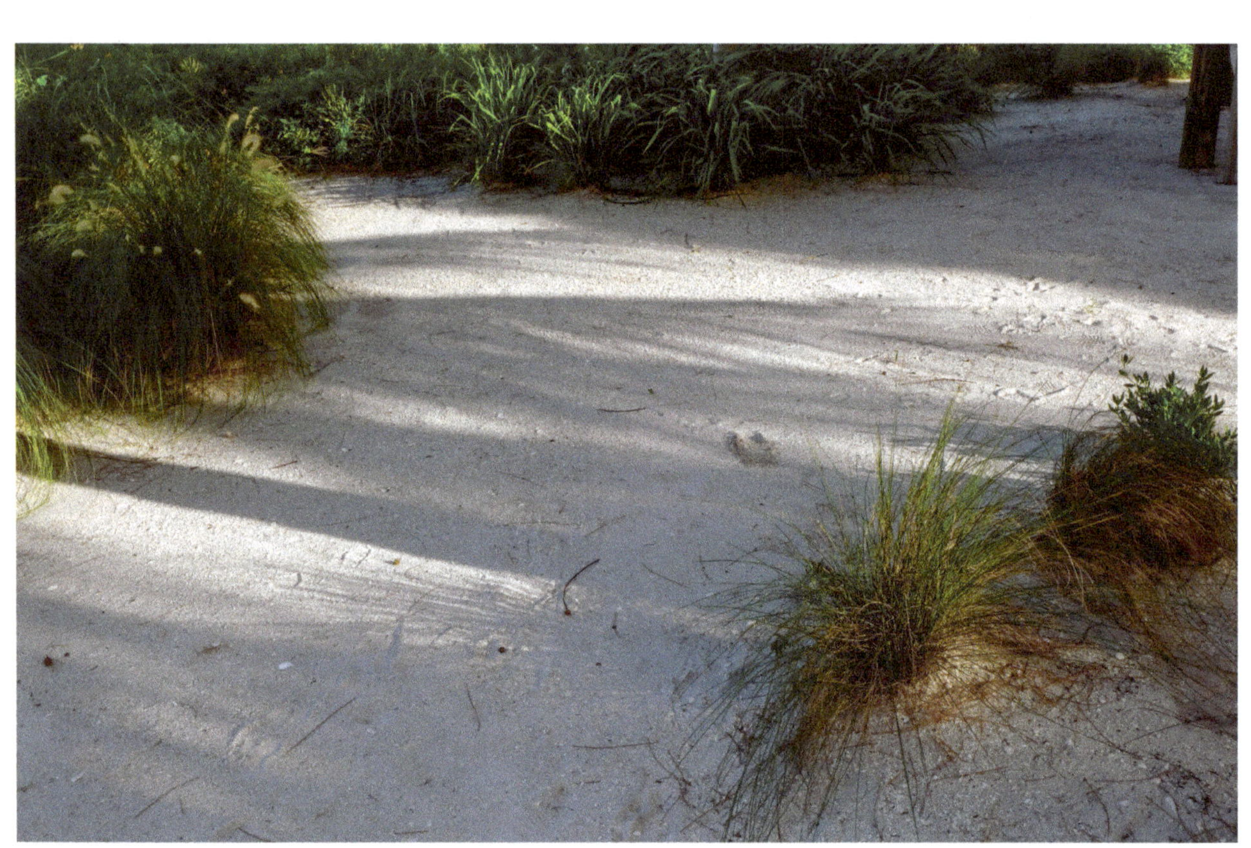

10/23

As sunrise
cracks day
open like
a clam,
the dog
in the yard
behind ours
obsesses
over his
fence, his
walk, the
ellipsis of
starlight. Listening
from our bed,
I agree to
everything.

10/24

Mexican daisies,
like Peter
Max sunrises,
swoon over
our patio.
The twilight
air is
cooler than
morning's. We
contemplate our
wins among
losses, the
world's and
ours. Cupped
in our hands,
wine winks
indifferently.

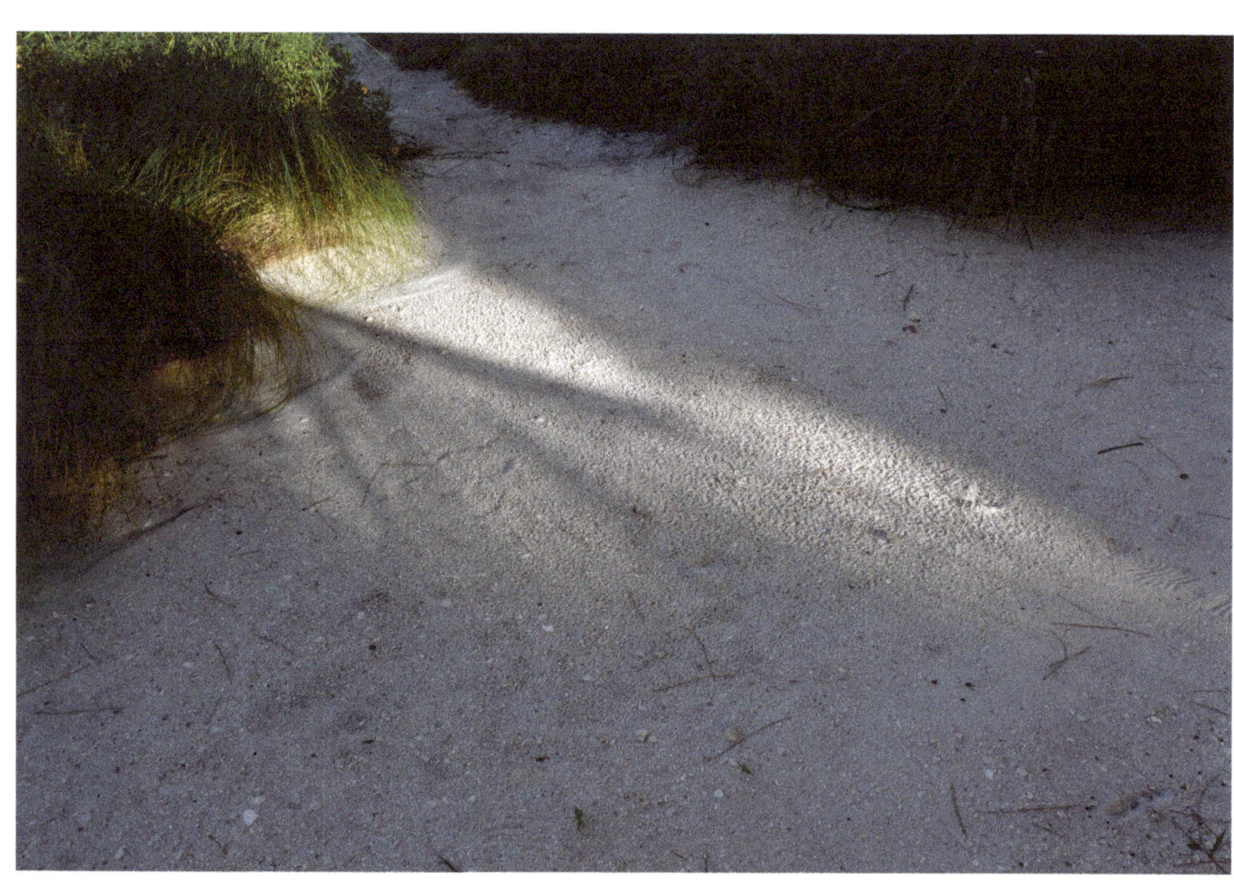

10/25

Cutting back
bleeding heart,
I mourn
the jumble
it once
was, its
valentines like
living bon-bons
cascading in
cherry and
cream. Now
neglected branches
scrape my
arms, regret's
scrawny limbs
scratch me
from the
root.

10/26

The canal
is tannic,
bedraggled. But
your crushed
shell patio,
green bananas,
flaming pentas
frame a
wonderstruck selfie
set. How
lucky we
are, together
again with
our memories,
your mimosas,
the plague
locked out
          for now.

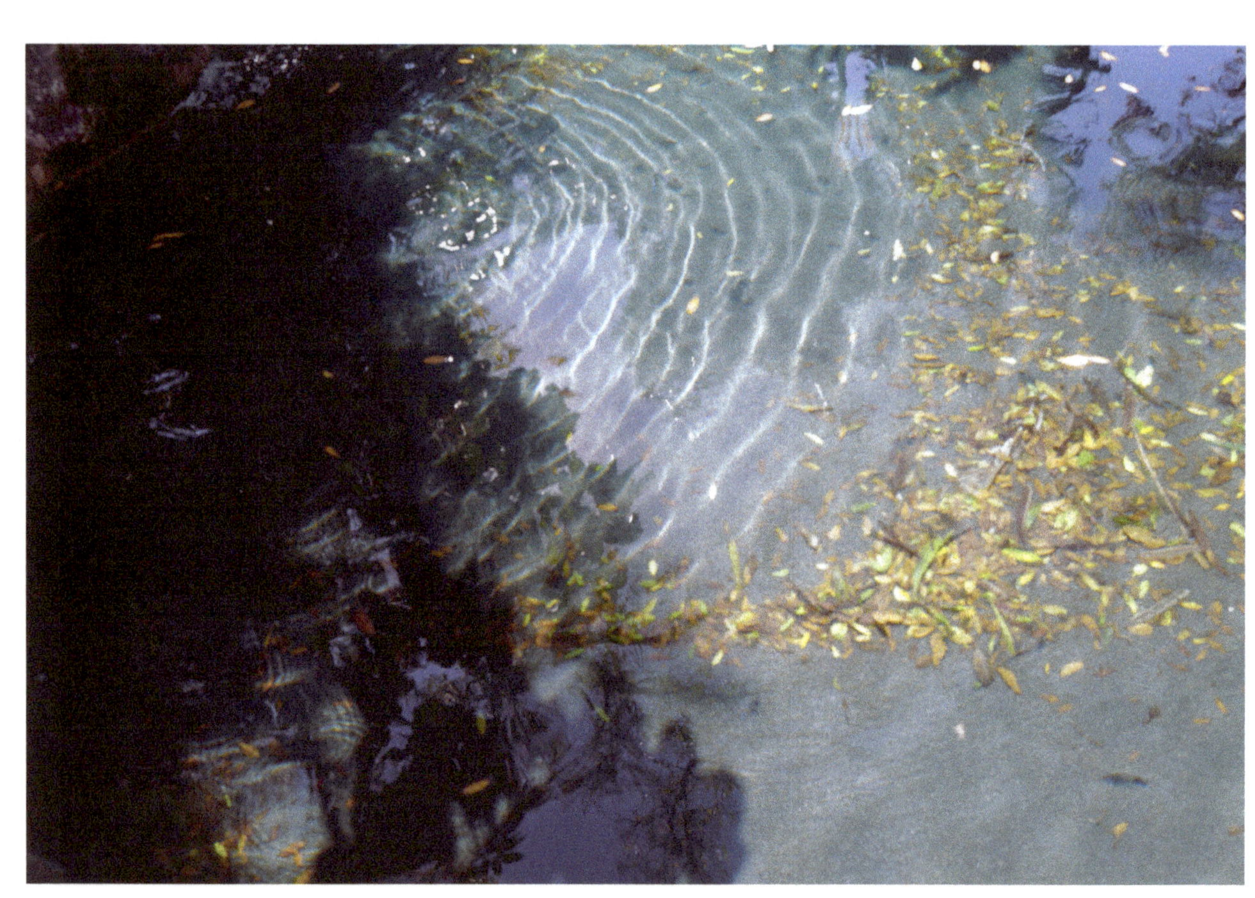

10/27

Anxiety rasps
the corners
of night.
The world
twitches, collapsed,
ravished by
upset. The
month has
a migraine
and dread
radiates across
my chest,
my brain.
Something
gaunt is
poking at
the window,
shoving us
awake.

10/28

Jolting us
from dreams,
guttering noises
outstrip the
streets—speed
racers slaying
blue neon.
I program
my phone
for muffled
rain, hoping.
But fire
trucks shriek
for hours,
demolishing
the app's
pretend
muted thunder
with real-life
death scenes.

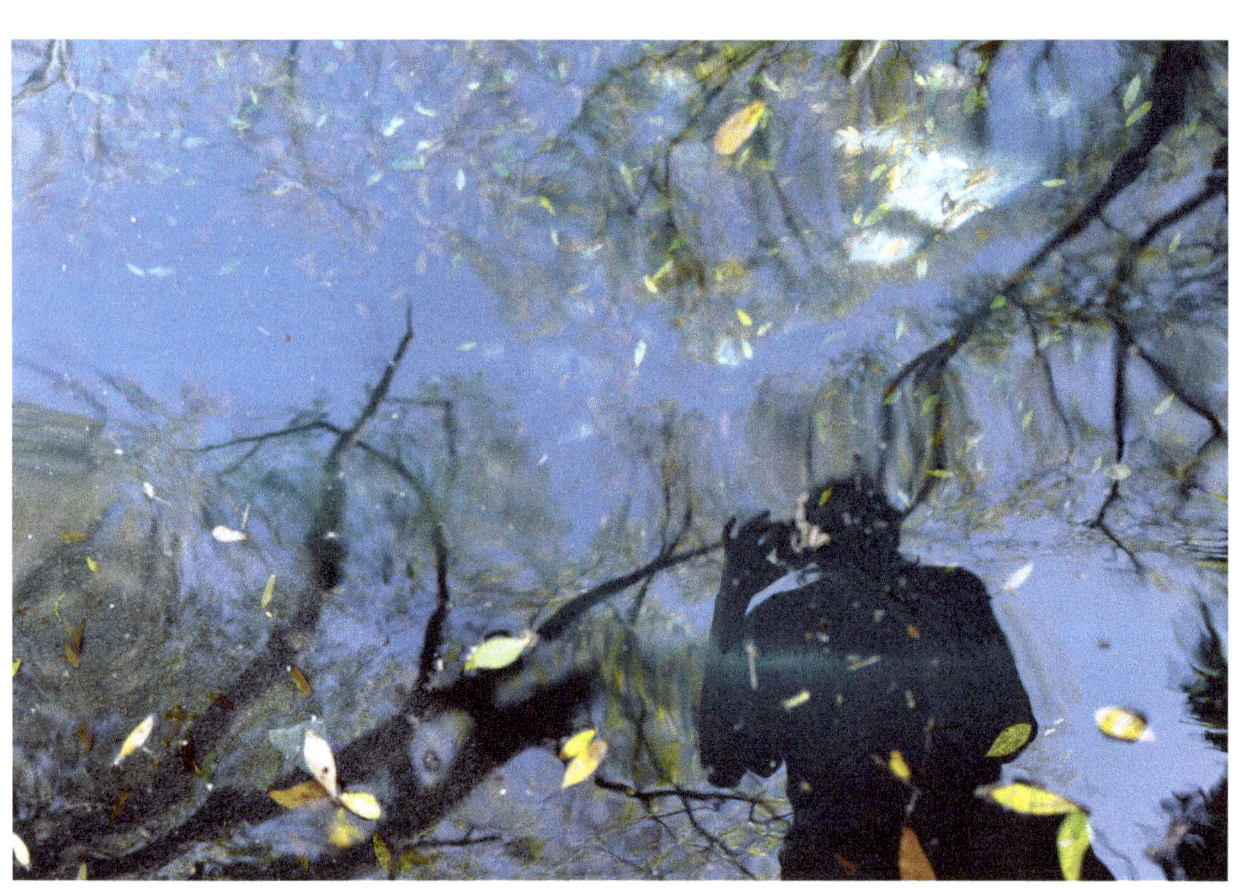

10/29

This plague
nearly buried
you. We
hear a
horror story
of gasps, tubes,
collapses,
a plea not
to die
in front of
your lover.
They turned
you face down
for nearly
a month,
the coma so
technicolor
you flew.

10/30

Don't be
scared when
you see
me, you
said. It's
been months.
Covid, your
captor's, finally
vanquished. *I*
look old,
lost my
hair. Then
you undo
the lock—
all I see is
you resurrected.
Your glinting
brilliant behind
your mask.

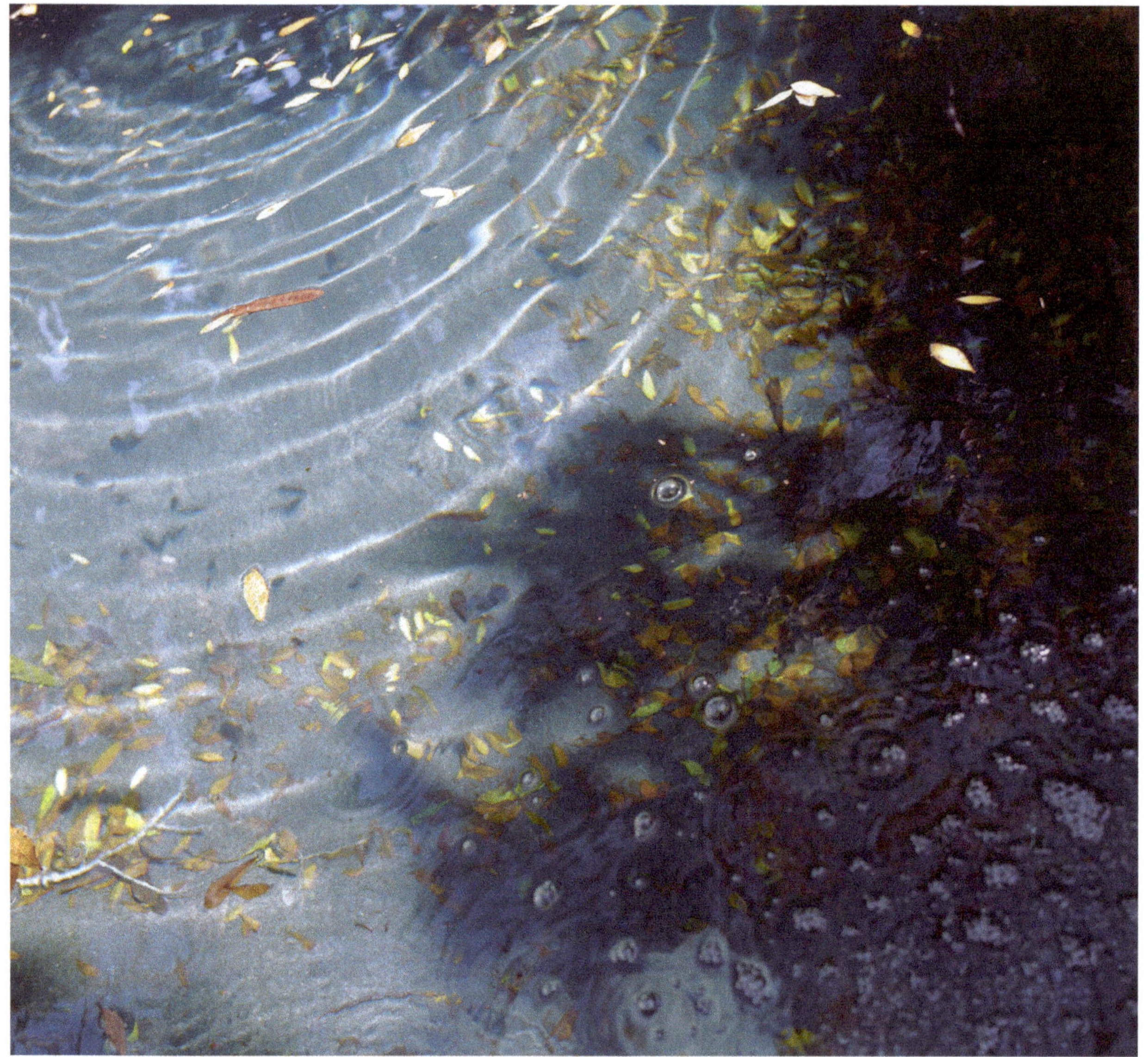

10/31

Blue moon,
platinum clouds.
Eyelash of
a ghost
in my palm.
Carved
radiance glimmers
down the
street. Let
me give
out only
sweetness to
this tricked-out
world: angel
breath to
sip, owl
song for
the heart,
a sugar
skull to
kiss.

November 2020

11/1

Sleepless hours.
Opening drapes
in other
rooms, I
disrobe a
dreamless moon.

11/2

Chrysanthemums,
death-cakes,
sugar skulls,
wine. All my
dust beloveds
rustle in
their frames.

11/3

Boarded store
fronts, guns
on alert.
Is this
really my
country, all
barrels aimed?

11/4

A bluejay
swiped her
wing across
the sky.
My heart
flits over
that prismic
pantomime.

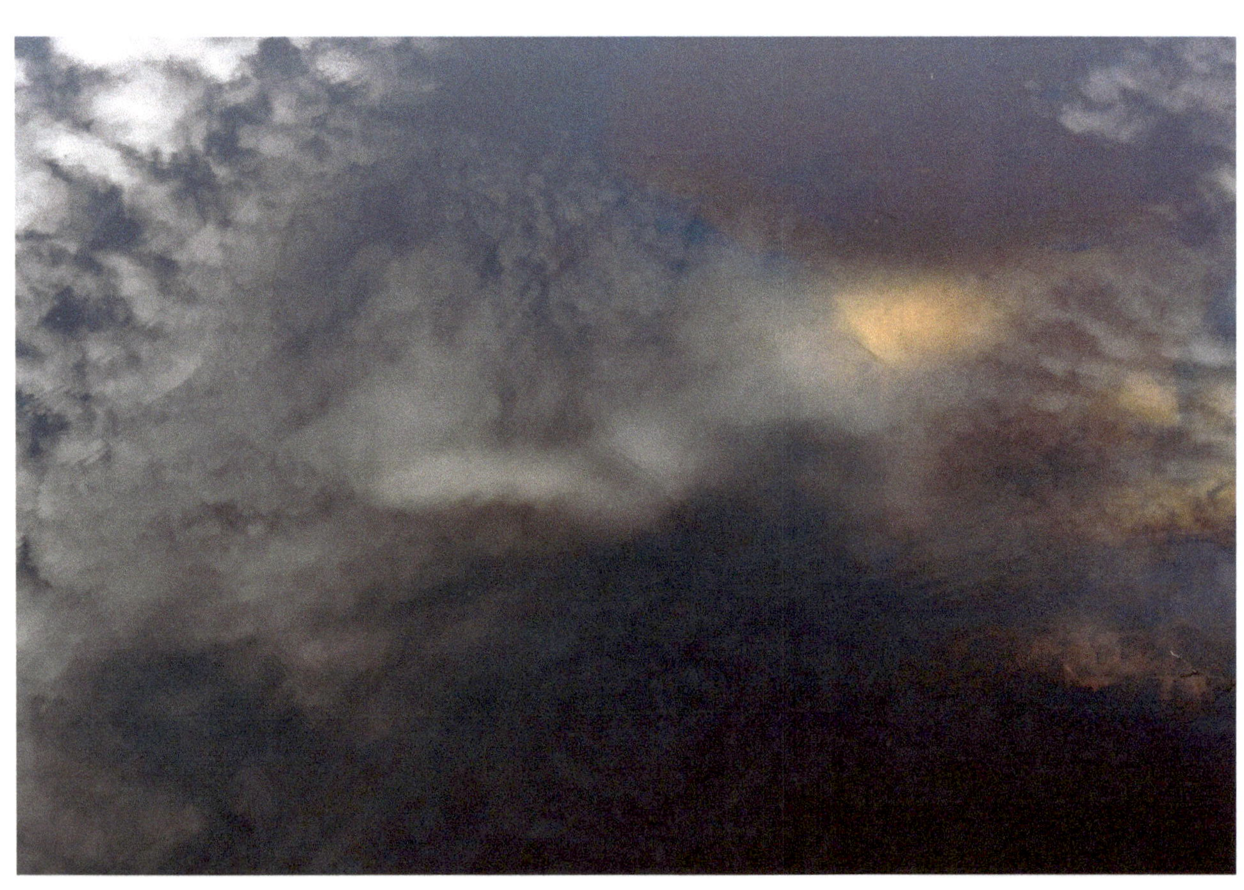

11/5

Sleepless, the
night before
the anniversary
of your
death, I
replay your
voice, my
heart stuttering.

11/6

Zoo wandering:
Florida panther
paces. The primates'
pontificating fills
the sky.
Our nation
waits, uncertain,
jumpy, uncaged.

11/8

We're
too relieved
to pay attention
to what's
barely contained,
seething, reptilian.
All day
we take
slow breaths
towards hope.

11/9

Twin sundogs
leap around
our kitchen.
Crystal snowdrops
fractal the
walls. Ravenous
for beauty,
our hungry
spirits lap
the light.

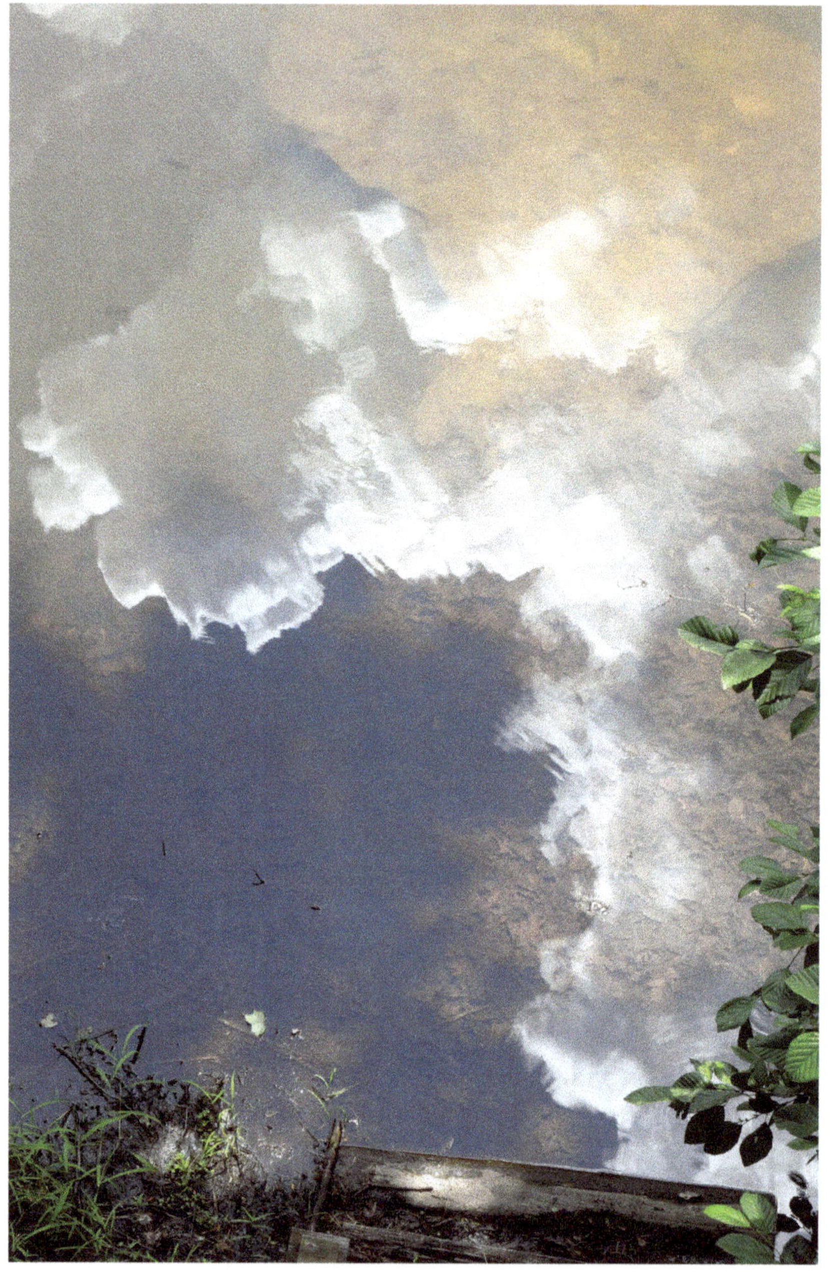

11/10

Crackling in
my ears,
my cottony
brain. Hip
and knee—
conjoined achiness.
Bereft of
words, my
aging body
explicates the
decades.

11/11

Moaning train
blurs the
dream. I
lurch into flaring
agitation, cellular
fidgeting, though
that whistle
is everything
yearning is,
taking me back.

11/12

A life-cracked
voice. Soul
music has
me couch
dancing, the
melody of
hand-outs and
rain. In
misty blues,
my first
self comes back.

11/13

Tin birds
clustered on
my wall,
wings pierced,
bodies hammered.
Their stop-timed
flight contrasts
with my
planetary heart—
full as
a murmuration
of sparrows.

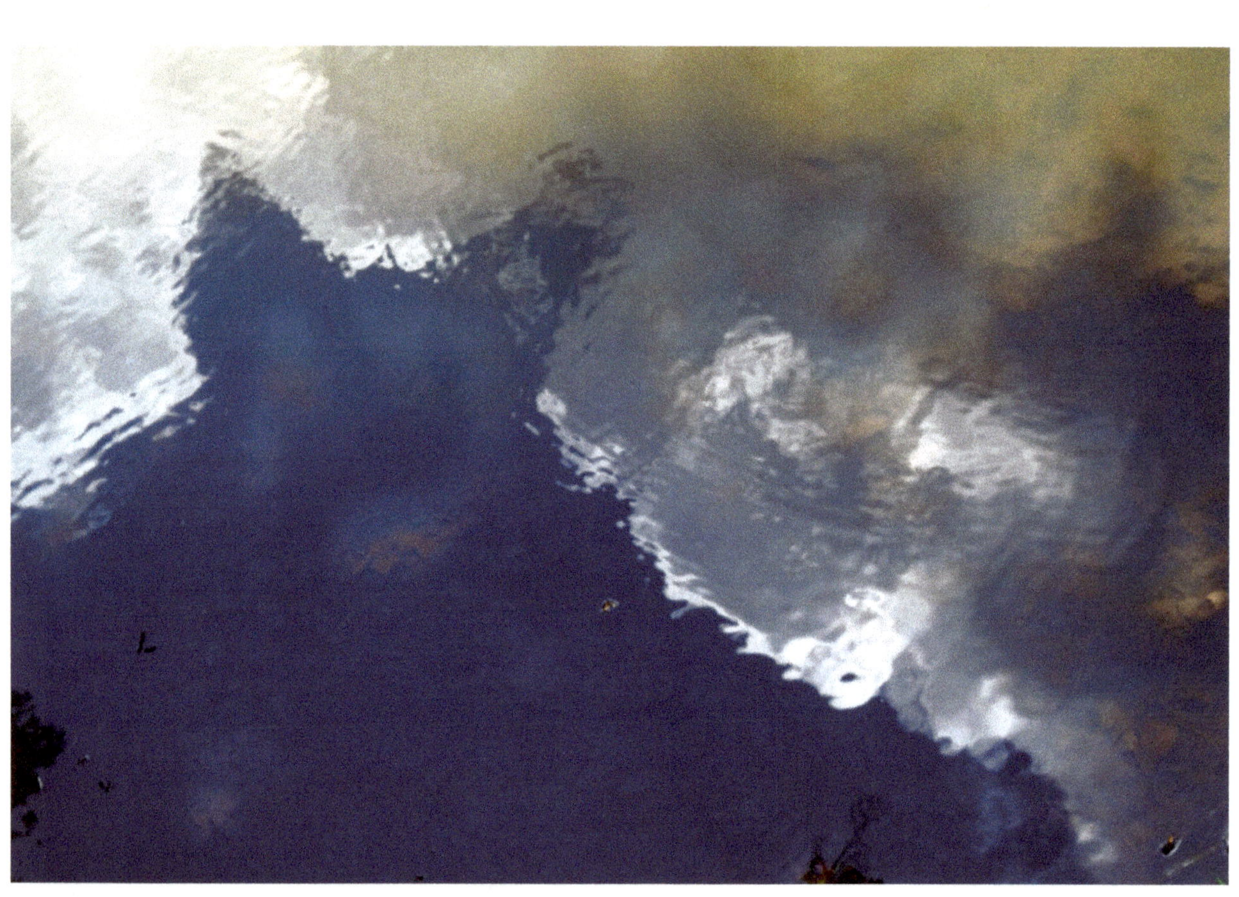

11/14

Sickness and
death lines
climb their
grim ladders.
We gamble
against risk,
eyeing grocery
shopping and
school days
like bullets.
Covid's gunning
for a
massacre.

11/16

One-eyed bully
with a crown
of poisoned thorns.
Choose your
prize: behind
door #1,
just fatigue.
#2, cough,
fever. #3
oxygen, intubation.
All the
others—death,
death.

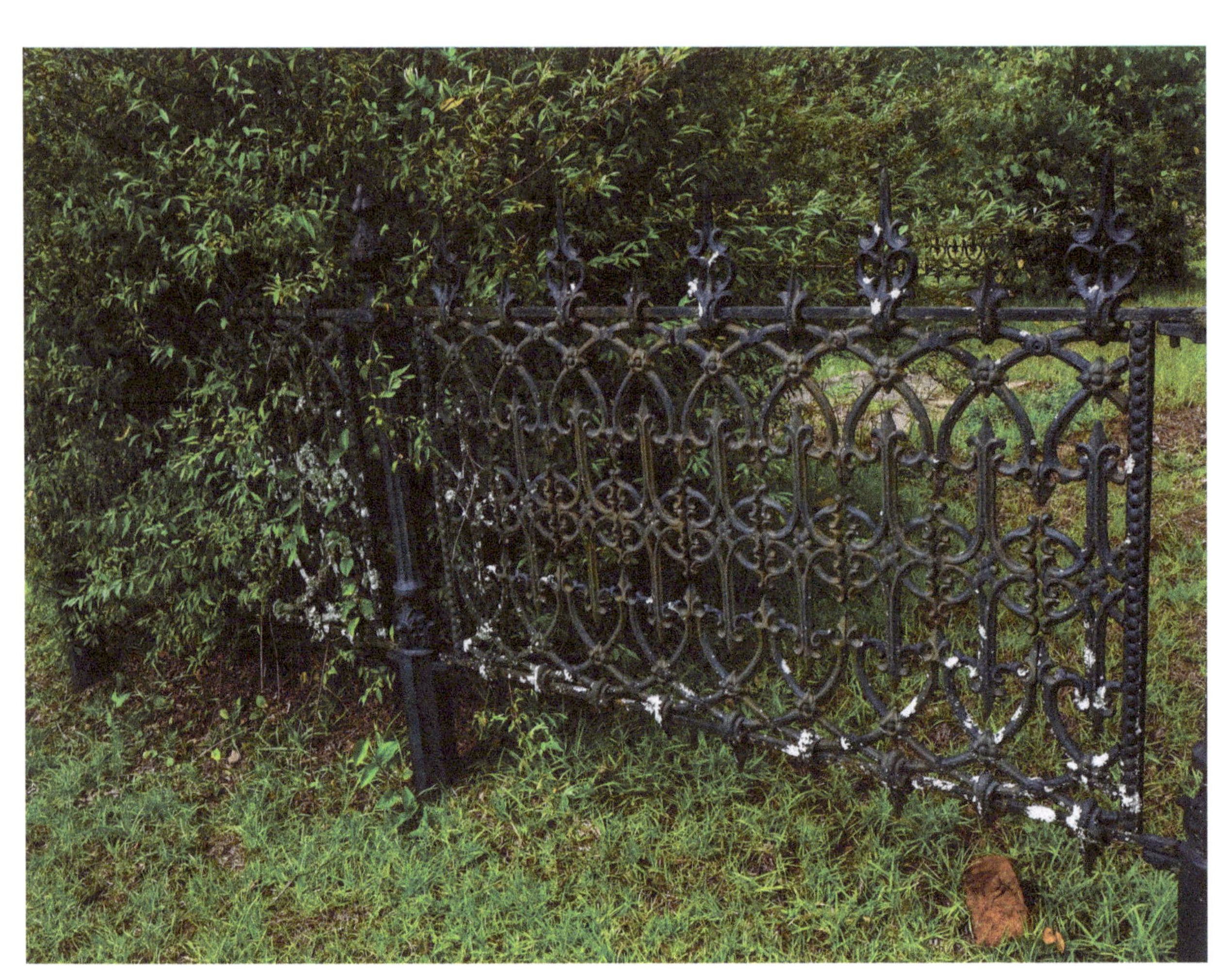

11/17

Trying, we
meet in
the garden
room, wicker
chairs distanced,
fans rotating.
Beyond this
green haven
silent stretchers
linger. We
sip sweet
wine, voices
vanishing in
the gloaming.

11/18

We sidestep
hugs like
awkward marionettes
as Covid
jerks, tightens
the strings.
People we
know are
rushed off
in a torrent
of sirens.
The lonesome
dead stack up.

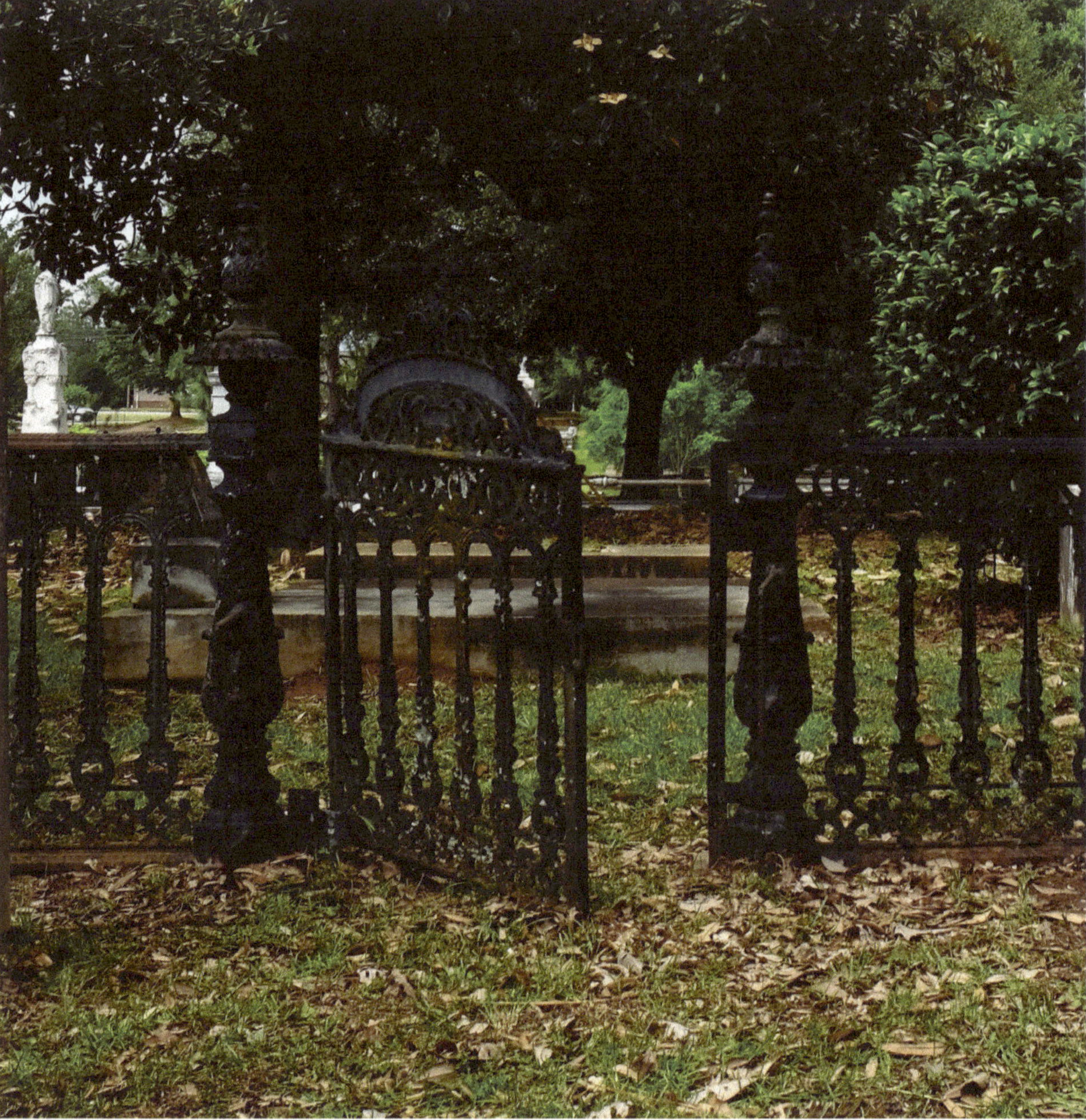

11/19

Days flip
over one
by one,
the escalating
charts and graphs
deadlier than
last week's.
We've shut
away song,
locked up
laughter. Our
once-exuberant voices
tiptoe across
open-windowed
tombs.

11/20

A quarter
million dead.
Doctors claim
we'll each
know hundreds
by the time
we're through.
Snares work
best when
the animal's
unaware of
them. That's
how we act,
the snare
tightening.

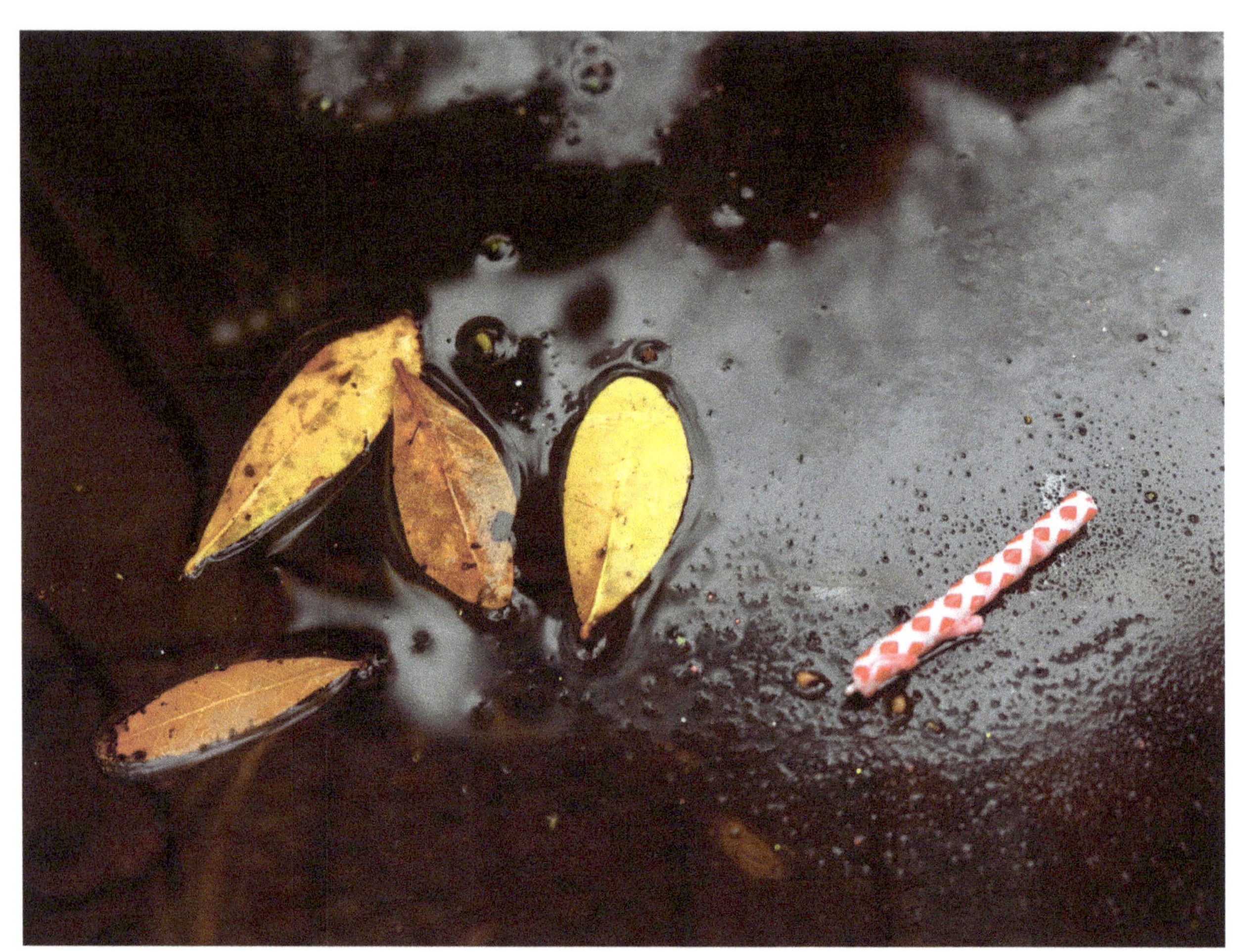

11/21

You've brought
us a dazzled
redbird
to serenade
our love.
A quarter
of a century—
we're
no longer
young. My
hair was
dark and
honeysuckle wild.
Yours skimmed
your shoulders,
feather-fine.

11/22

Our starfish
life: years
ebb in
velvet wavelets,
churning tempests.
Let not
to the marriage
of true minds . . .
Coral mornings
you make
coffee, I,
French toast.
Our gifts:
silver posy
love, bracelets,
sonnet-spun.

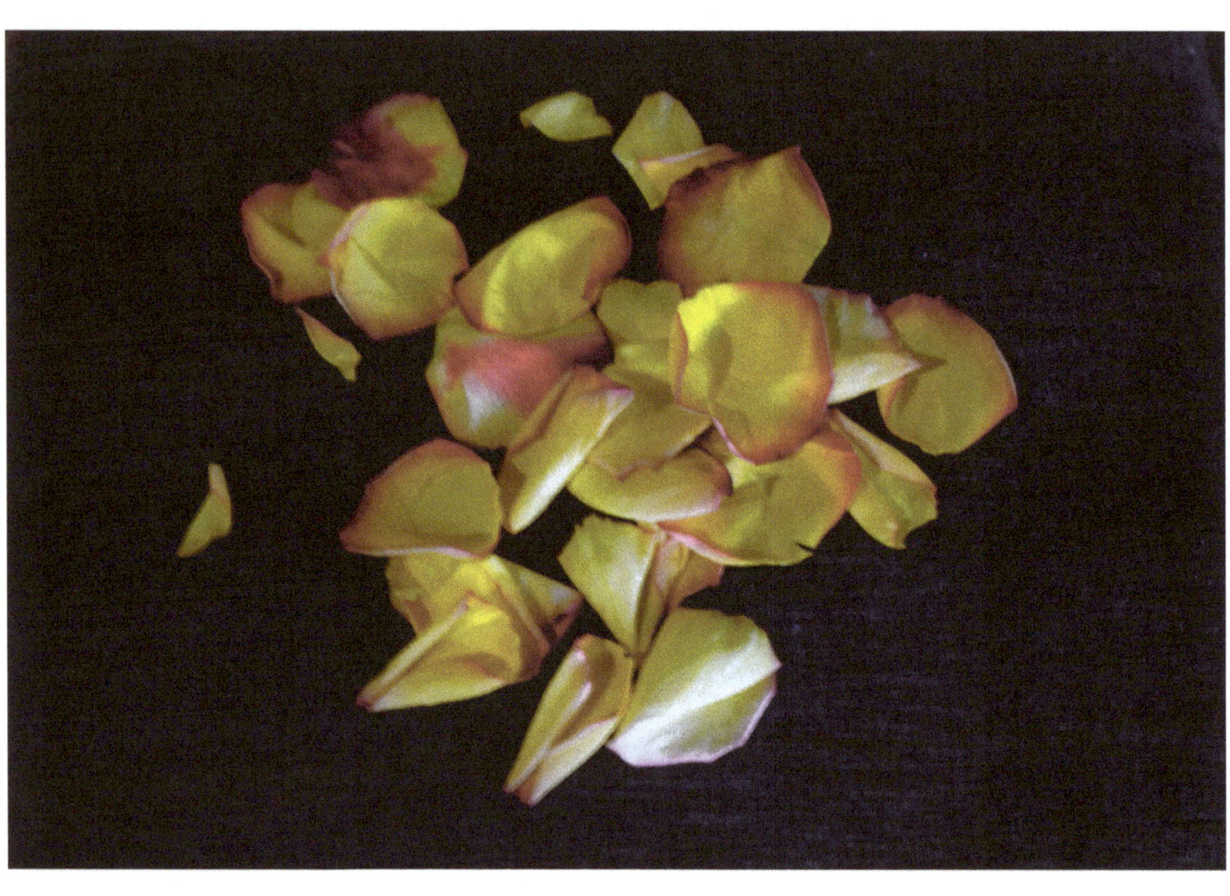

11/23

Tassels of
sunlight sway
over the
lawn. Fall's
finally lit
its elf-light,
unmasked its
silk-faced coolness.
The virus
rages, ravaging
the land
street by
street. We
rest in
the dappling,
holding hands,
momentary refugees.

11/24

I wipe
all my
windows to
glinting. From
inside, we
witness the
jumbled slipstream
of oldsters
resisting restaurants,
youngsters insistent
on crowd-dazzle.
No one
knows where
the lung-
butcher lurks
indiscriminate as
blow flies
swarming.

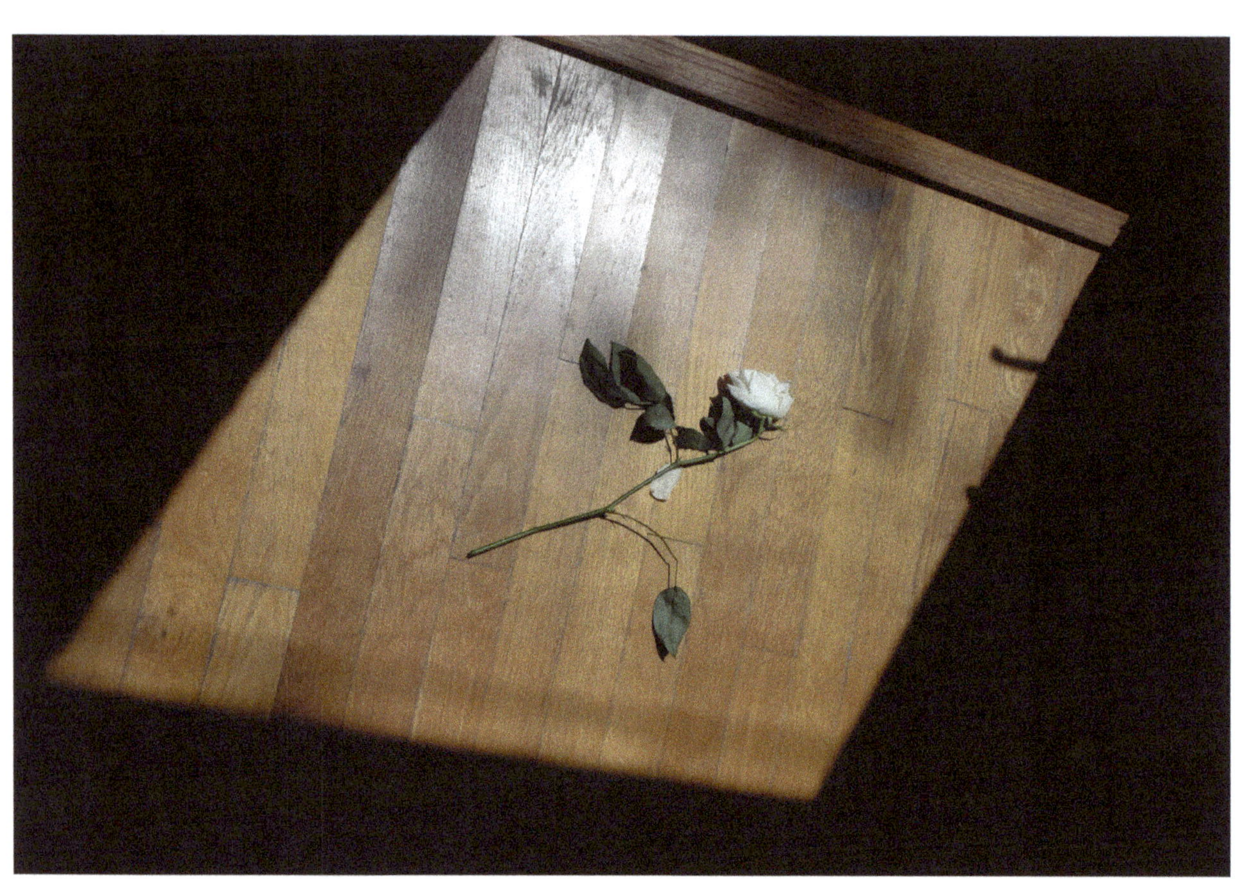

11/25

I gild
the lily,
cleaning even
crusted candle
holders, baseboard
corners, dusty
bottle tops
shouldering across
the makeshift
bar. Meanwhile
the world
is riven.
Gleam, glow
glimmer: I
push back
gloom, take
the others
to heart.

11/26

Our year
of misery.
Yet, my
friend's lambent
porch light
welcomes me.
My sisters'
laughter conjures
mine, confetti-like.
My sons'
smiles balloon
with mama-love.
Even in
sleep, my
husband's hands
find mine.
Like chrysanthemum
petals, gratitude
unfurls.

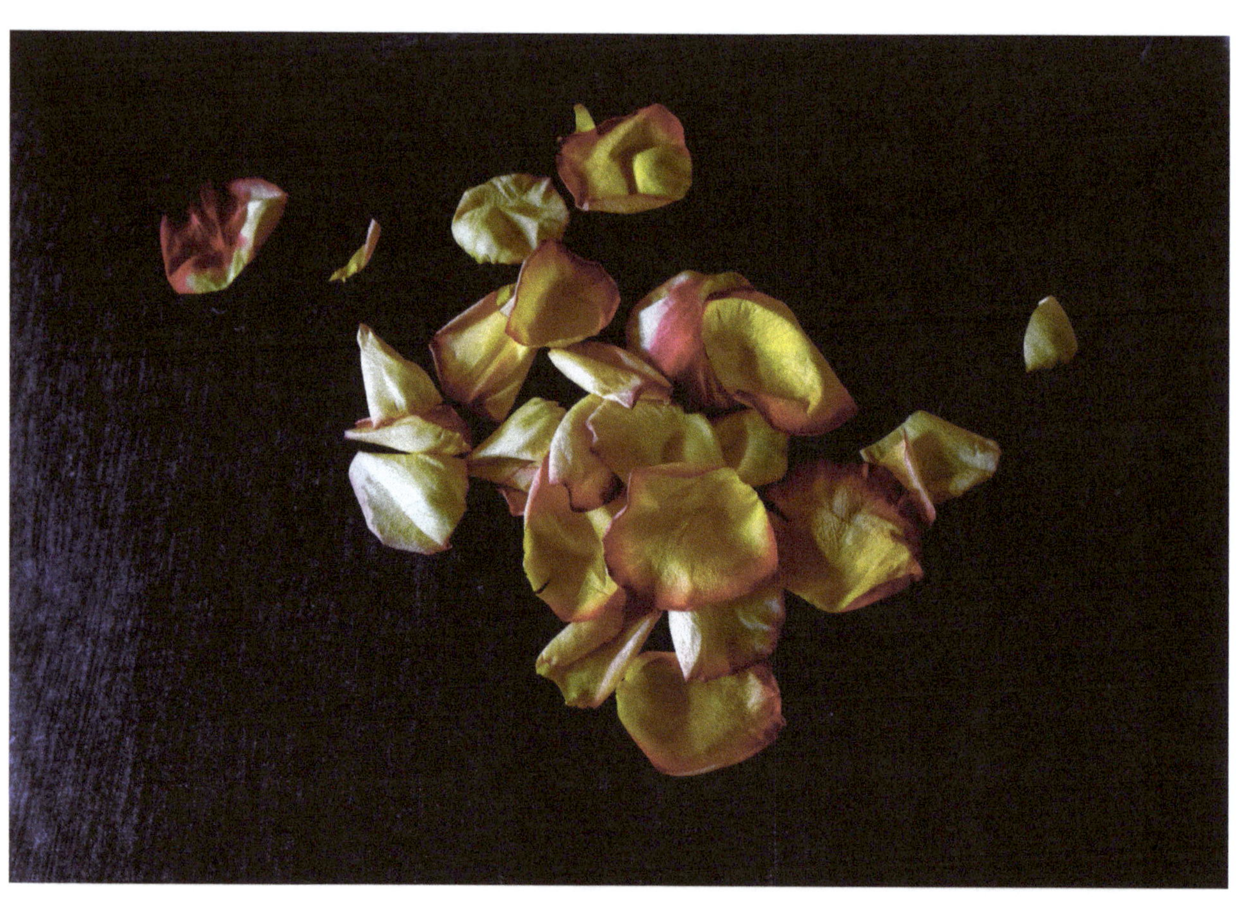

11/27

Childhood Thanksgivings:
Grandmama's sideboard
bench-pressed ham
on one end,
turkey on
the other.
In between—
candied yams,
chestnuts,
giblet gravy.
Bourbon soaked
the fruitcake
cheesecloth. But
no liquor
for us, just
ambrosia: Florida
oranges making
us light-hearted,
giddy.

11/28

Sterling silver
spoons glisten
the table
in a jubilant
archipelago.
Cream and
sugar bowl
glimmer, exultant
silver apples.
Polished pitchers,
trays, candlesticks,
butter knives
glinting like
stilled lightning.
The centerpiece,
candlelight in
bloom. My
love's party
face out-glittering
everything.

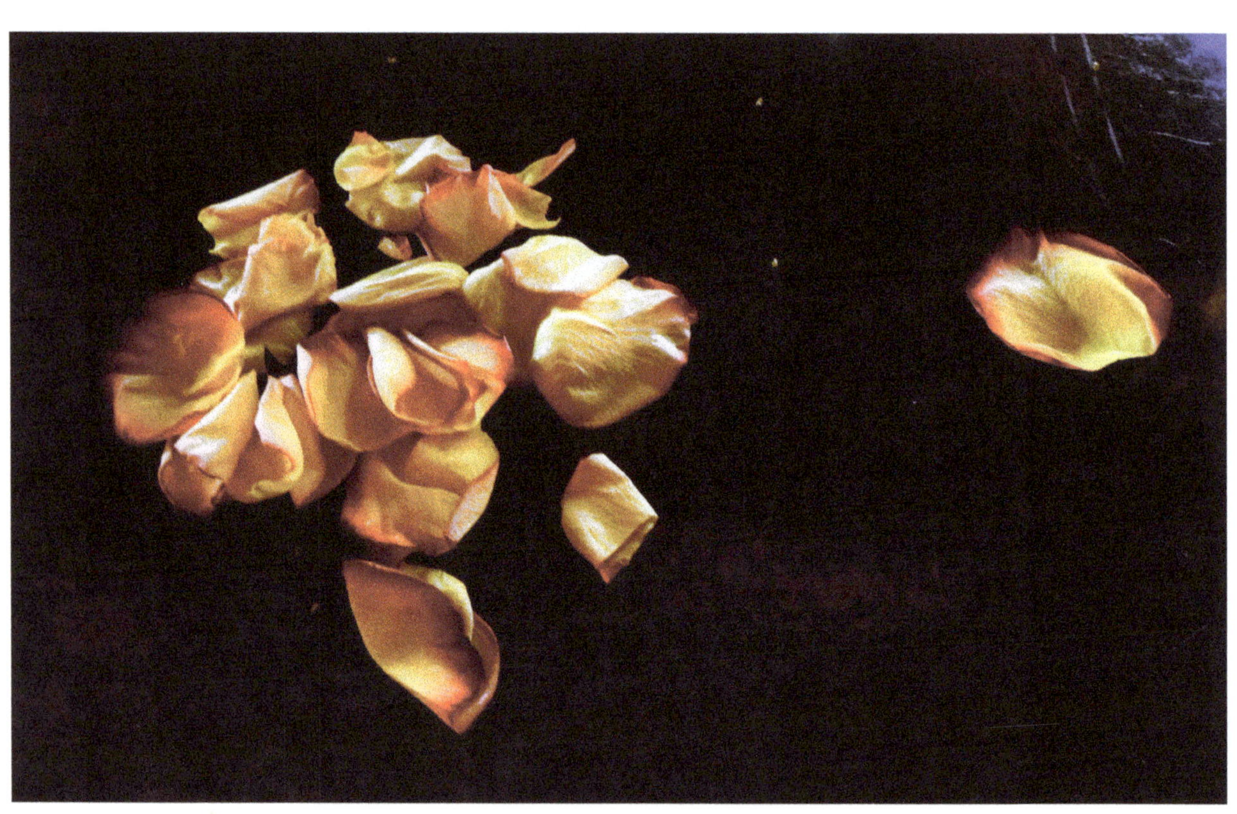

11/29

Fold up
the borrowed
tables. Unstring
the garden
lights. Was
it worth
it? Stuff
tablecloths into
the washer.
Count the
silver, spot
clean napkins.
Wash the
china by
hand. Feel
like you're
made today
both of
lost gardenias
and mother-of-pearl.

11/30

I'm locking
the gate
on this
month like
plague-ridden peasants
barring the
town wall.
Here's a
psychic deadbolt
against brass-
knuckle politics
and spiraling
mortal numbers.
Souls
float up
like emoji
hearts. The
raw, wretched
bruising
transforms into
a harvest moon.

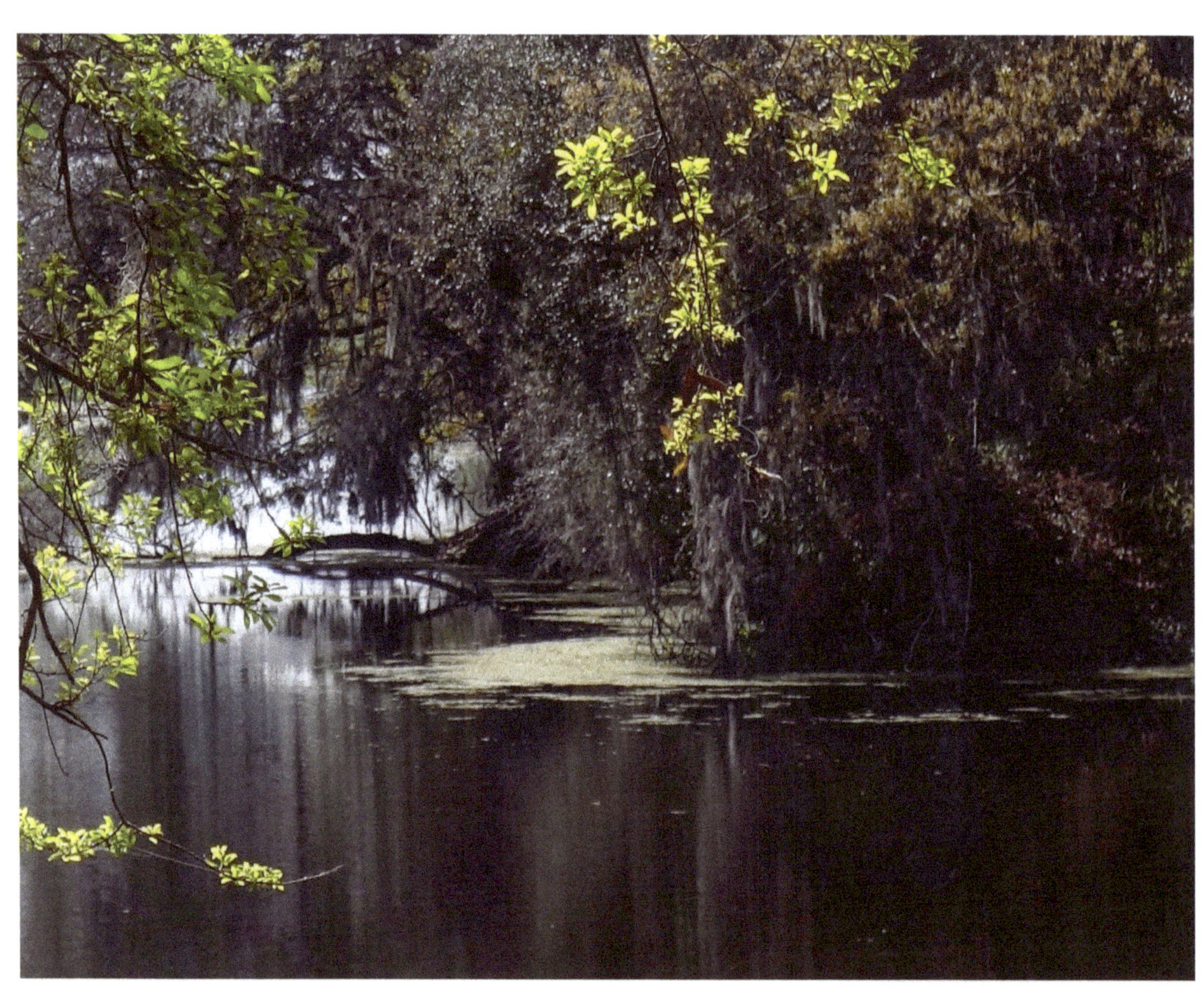

December 2020

12/1

Migrating
crows chatter
the month's
commencement.
Winter solstice
rocks awake
on cardinal
wings.

12/2

Cold this
morning, like
childhood's frost,
the crackling
grass. Memory's
chilly glove
fits fine.

12/3

First wintery
night—the
heat's gone
out. We
shiver in
front of
the thermostat,
laughing.

12/4

Desperate for
calm, we
walk into
soft-spectrumed twilight.
Early Venus
eavesdrops on
our gratitude
and woes.

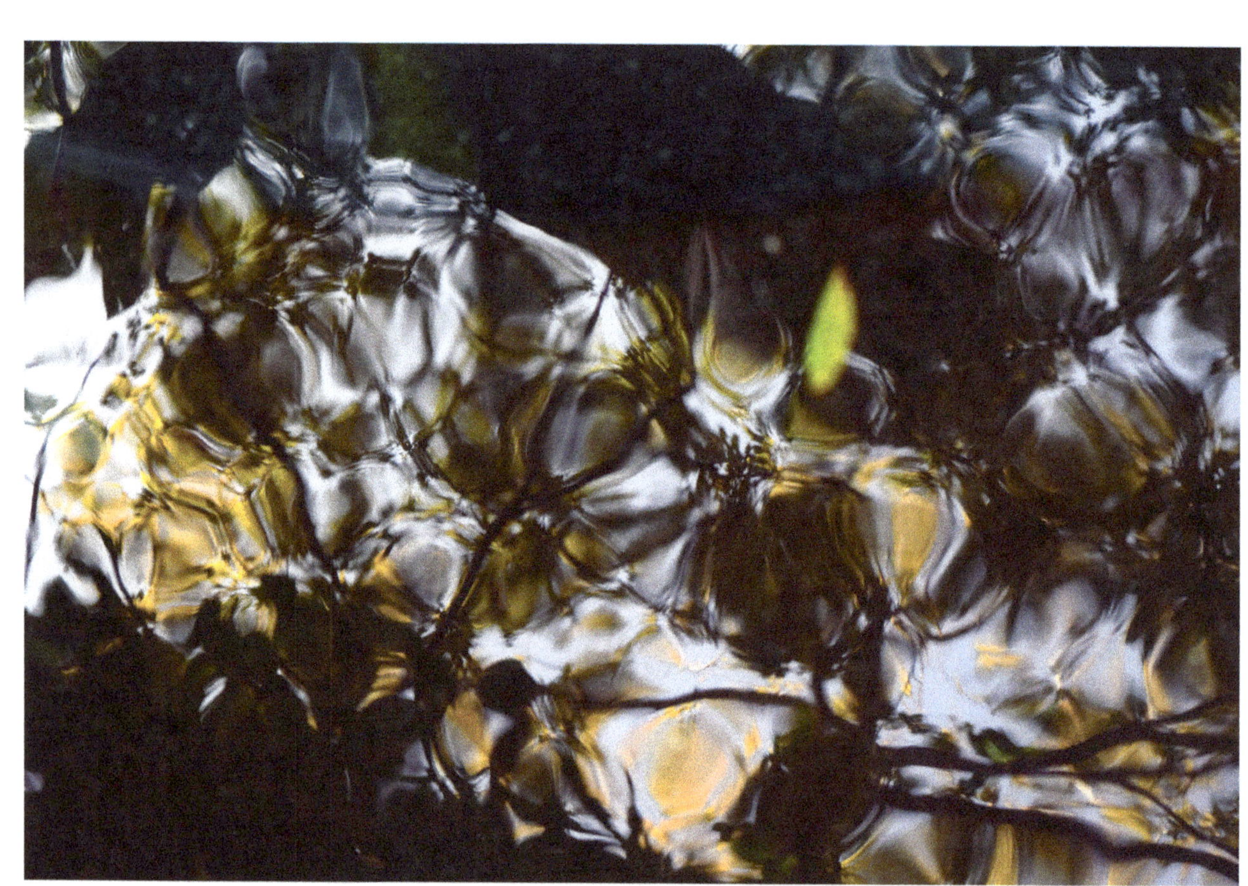

12/5

The night
sky's on
Twitter. I'm
not. Blocking
streetlights, I
fall up
into the
meadow
of stars.

12/7

Around Lake
Roberta, whistling
ducks balance
on one
leg. Unlike
us, they're
perfectly steady
as night-slivering
rain barges in.

12/8

In the
parking lot,
Santa waves
tentative cars
towards stacks
of boxed
cans, lumpy
bags. The
long weary
line crawls.

12/9

Their mom
lugs the
cart from
the distribution
tent. Just
enough for this
week. They
fidget by
the van,
trunk empty.

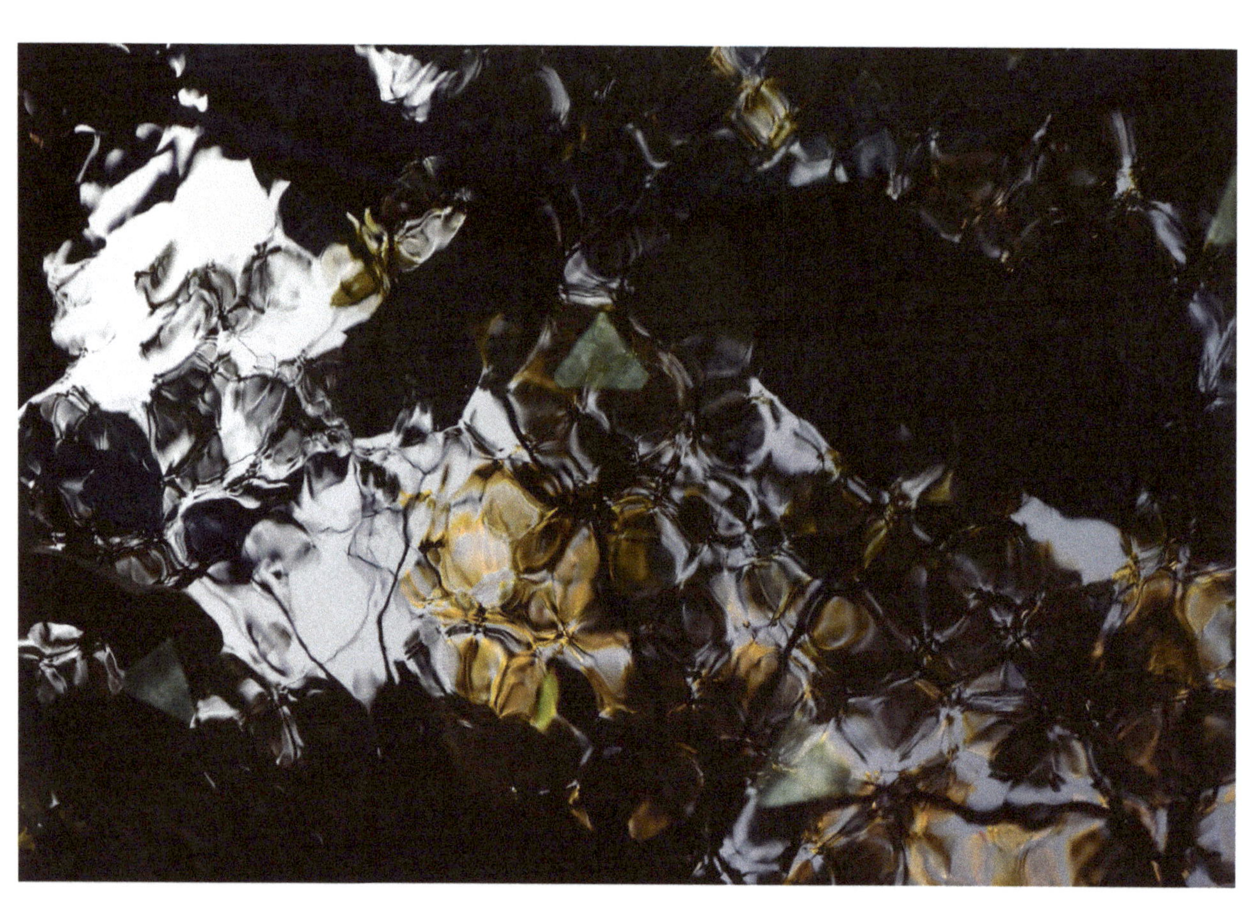

12/10

Blue gloves
and masks
pantomime our
holiday caresses.
We hold
back love
just enough.
Windblown roses
mimic the
frisson of
a kiss.

12/11

In our
minds, we
storyboard virus
scenarios. The
photo of
our friend—
tied down,
intubated—flashes:
the strangled
trailer for
a gasping
film.

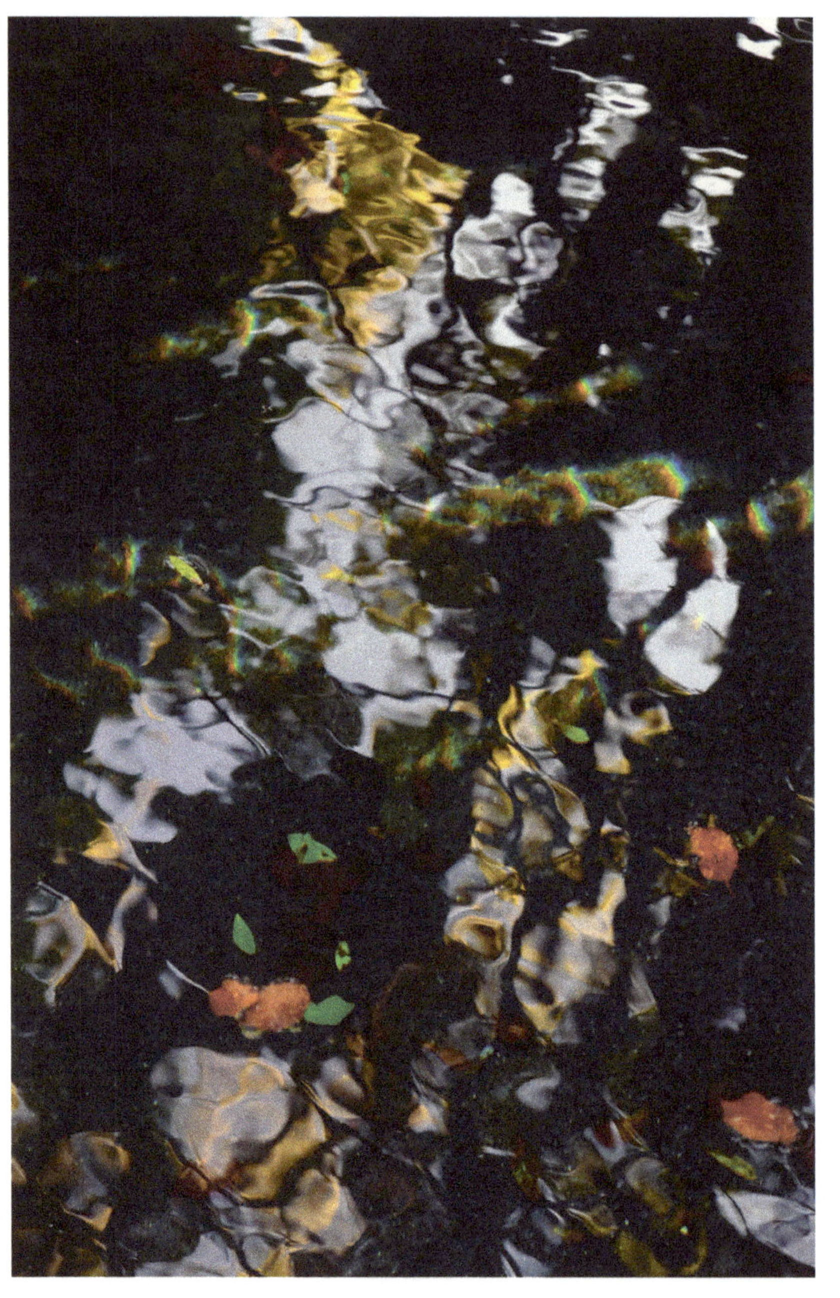

12/12

Do you
feel anxious,
fatigued, have
trouble sleeping?
Unable to
concentrate? Afraid
to leave
the house?
Are you
sad? Depressed?
Feeling hopeless?
Are you?

12/13

3,000 dead
in one
day. As
we part
with our
fist bumps,
air hugs,
my friend
tells me
about two
we both
know. Both
knew.

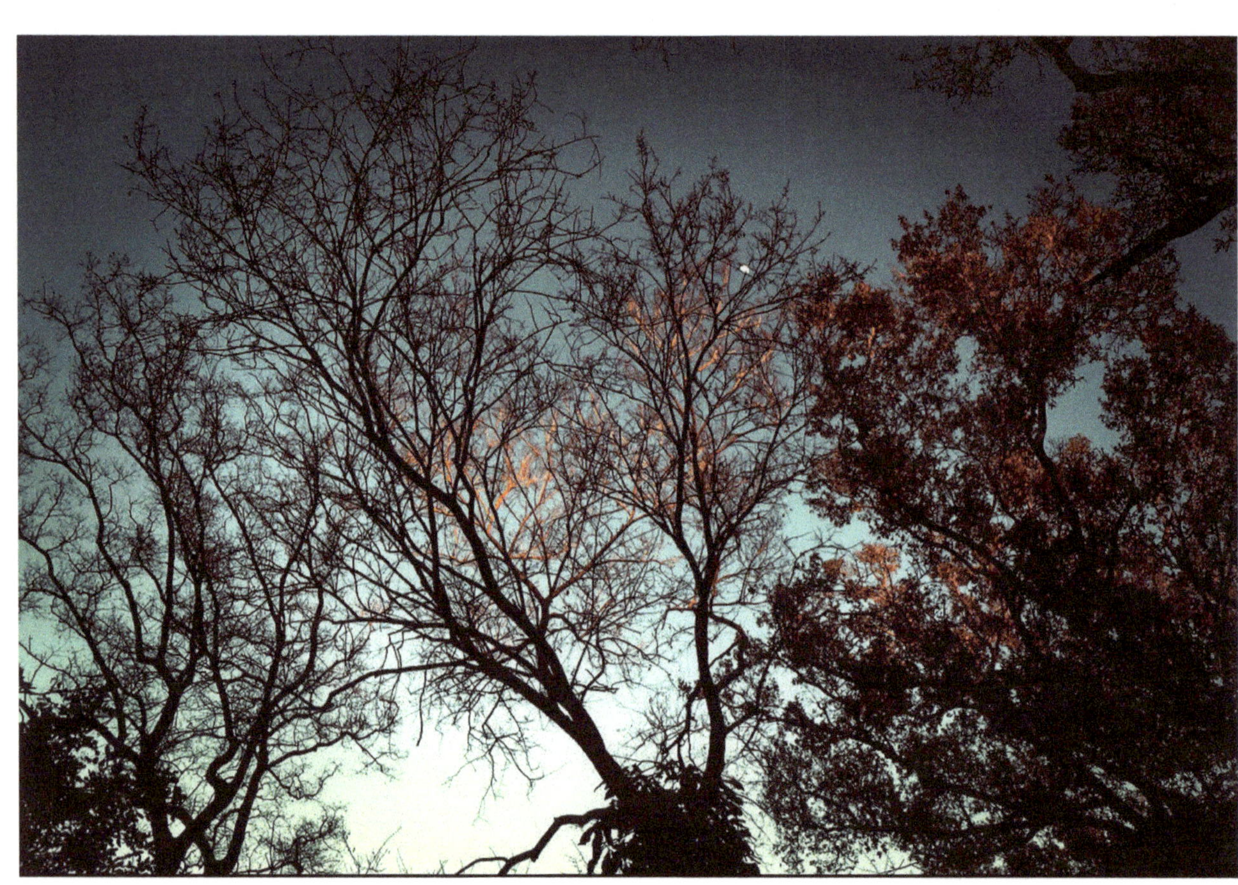

12/15

Poems float
like dust
motes, ready
for the
plucking. But
today my
stiff fingers
pinch only
awful headlines
I can't
write about,
the day
itself a
ghost.

12/16

The ninety-year-
old dons
her bravura,
presents her
bicep to
the vaccine
syringe. She
stares straight
ahead, a
fighter's stare
shoving outwitted
death back
into his
wheezing corner.

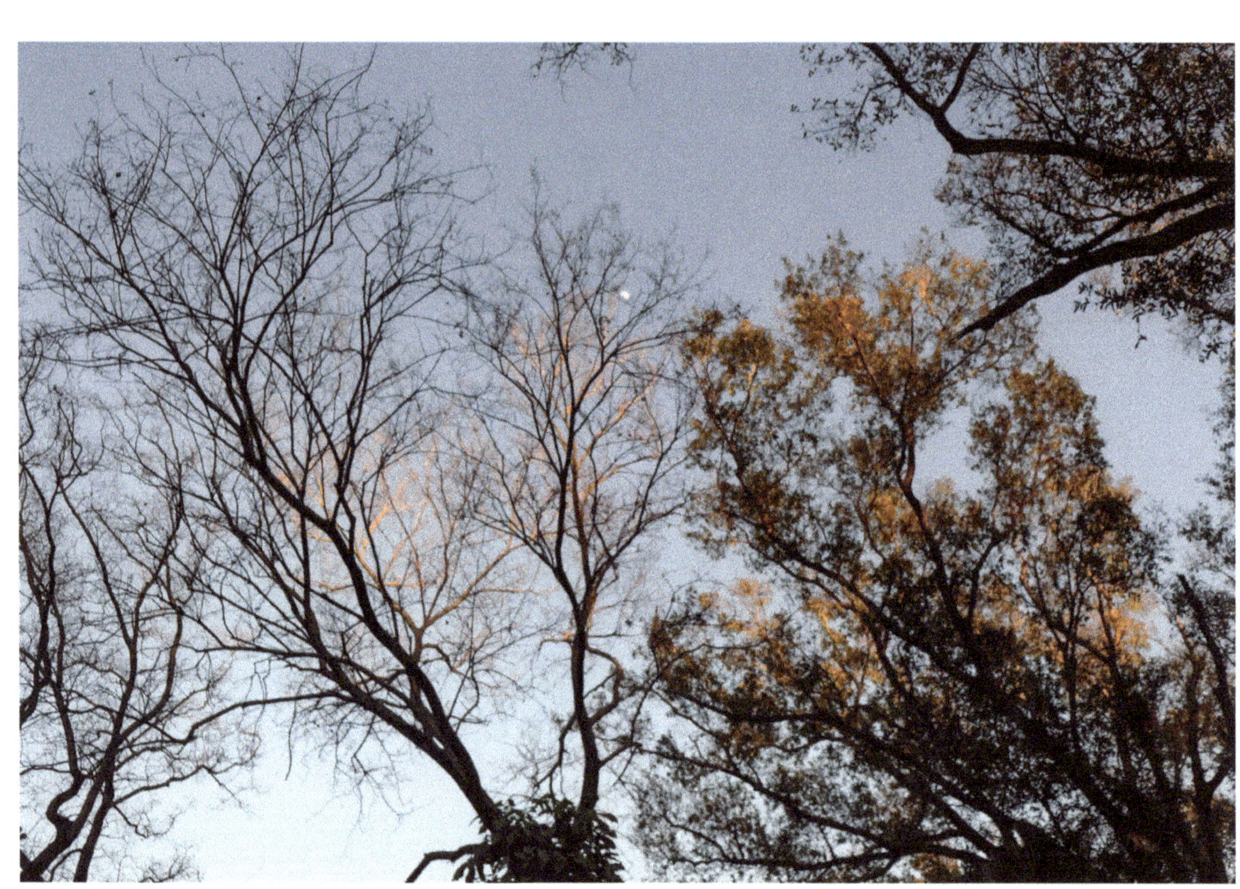

12/17

The holiday's
shrunken. At
first I
think prunes,
but that's
not it.
No, the season's
marzipan,
the days
in their
December box
shimmering green,
gold, blush-rose.

12/18

Plump presents:
Mom's handwritten
recipes, inside
tips. For
cheese-and-date pastries
she wrote:
My Mama.
For ricotta
cookies: *Dad's
favorite.* My
eyes gobble
the letters.
As if sugar
makes Christmas
Christmas.

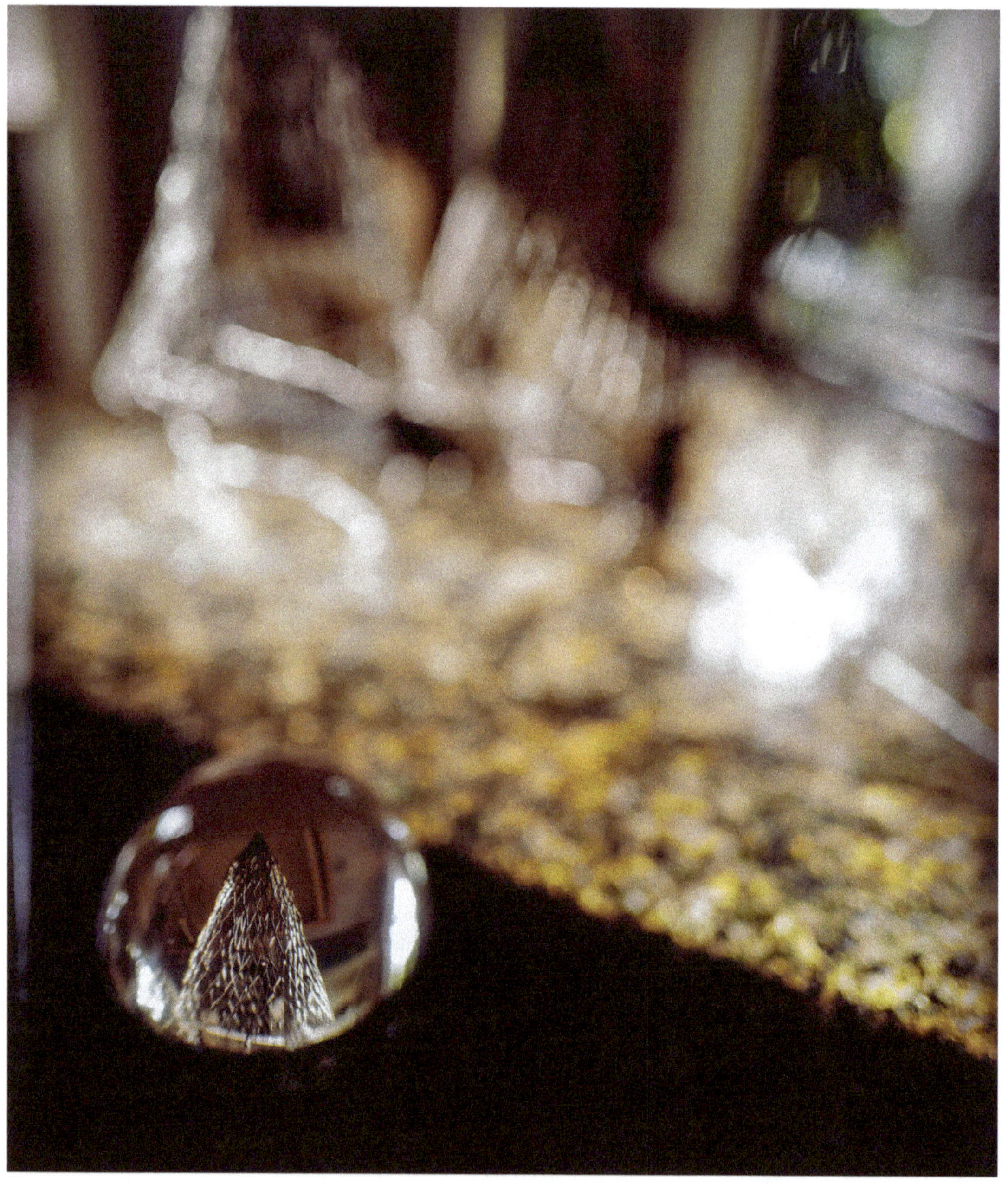

12/19

I'm not
really a
Christmas song
girl, DJ
Joellen says,
coaxing the
airwaves into
a firelight
croon. My
car fills
with alto
glow-notes, tinselly
vibrato. Humming,
I unreel
my parents'
harmony.

12/20

On its
mechanical stand,
the tree
revolves in
wonder, bareness,
a metaphor
for time.
Glimpses between
twinkling: a
thumb-sized elf,
glass cardinal,
lacy angel
bringing back
our parents,
then turning.
away.

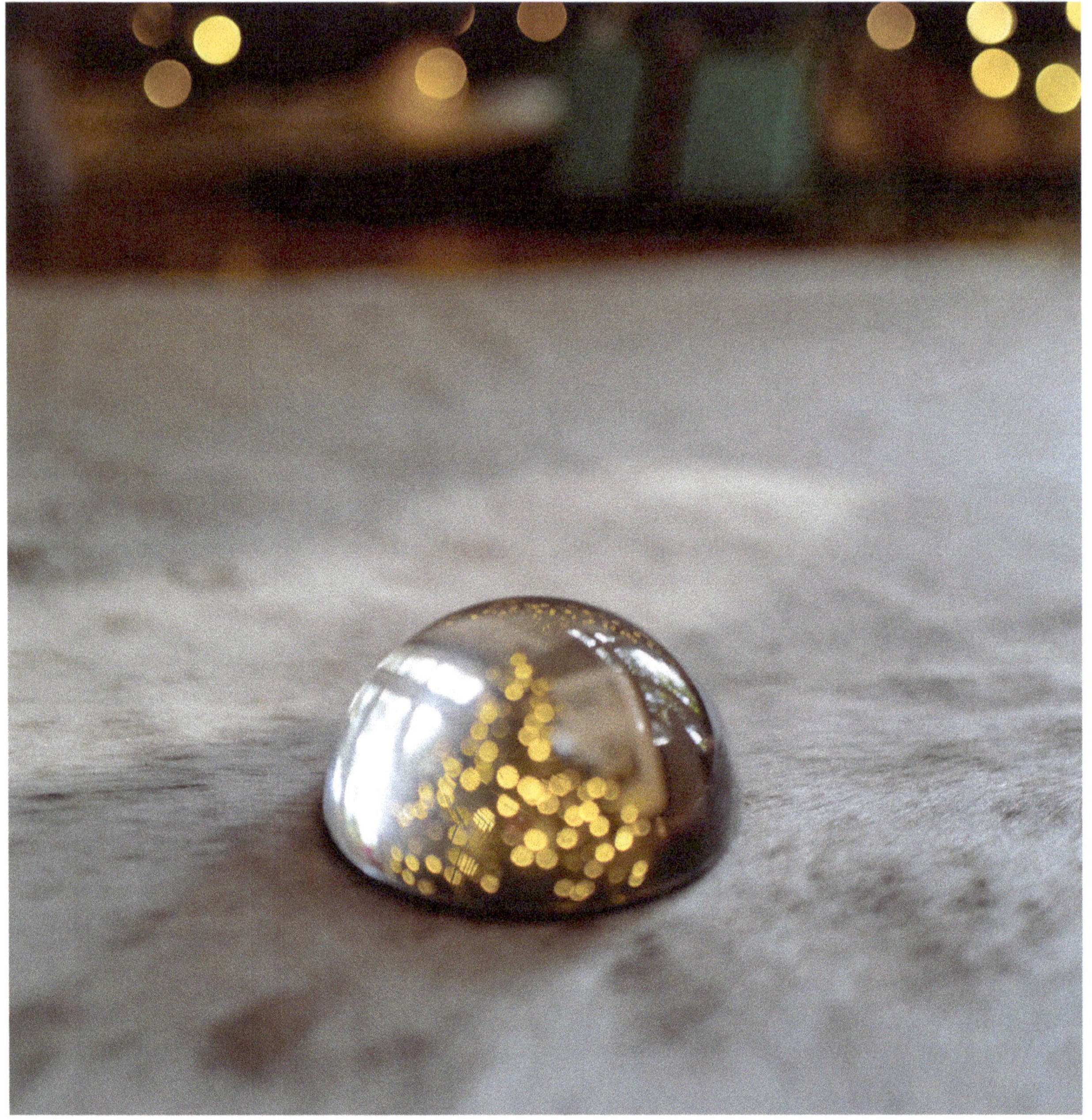

12/21

He'd slept
on Nebraska
Avenue. She
was company.
I trailed
their voices
around Lake
Roberta, passing
with *hello.*
He called,
This is
just breathtaking!
A heron
glided over
isinglassed water
as the homeless
and I
shared beauty.

12/22

Rising on
stacked up
centuries, Jupiter
and Saturn
show off
their Christmas
embrace. In
a dusk-dark
hay field,
the telescope
shivers while
we vie
to witness
history clasp
the glittering
velvet vault.

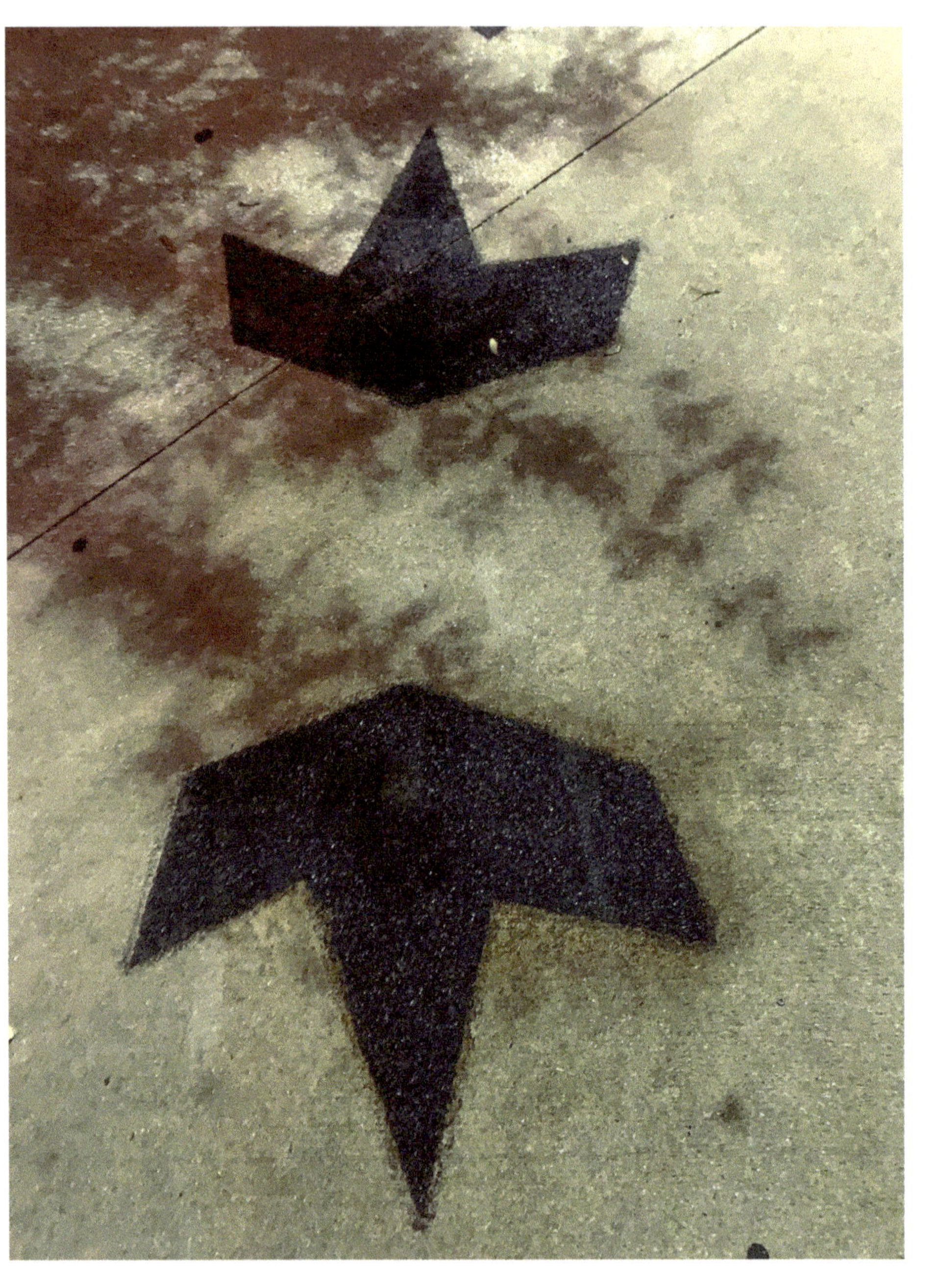

12/23

I've been
tussling with
Christmas spirit,
pushing bad
news down
a well.
I've tried
drowning it
each morning,
but it
keeps gushing
up. Comfort
and joy
are phosphorescent,
but I'm
holding sludge
in my arms.

12/24

We start
with masks
on, our
starved gladness
staggering across
the rooms,
air-kissing
beloveds who've
travelled for
this gift-giving
fête. Later,
we ditch
the masks,
hold hands.
Singing "Silent
Night," we
pray hard
and worry.

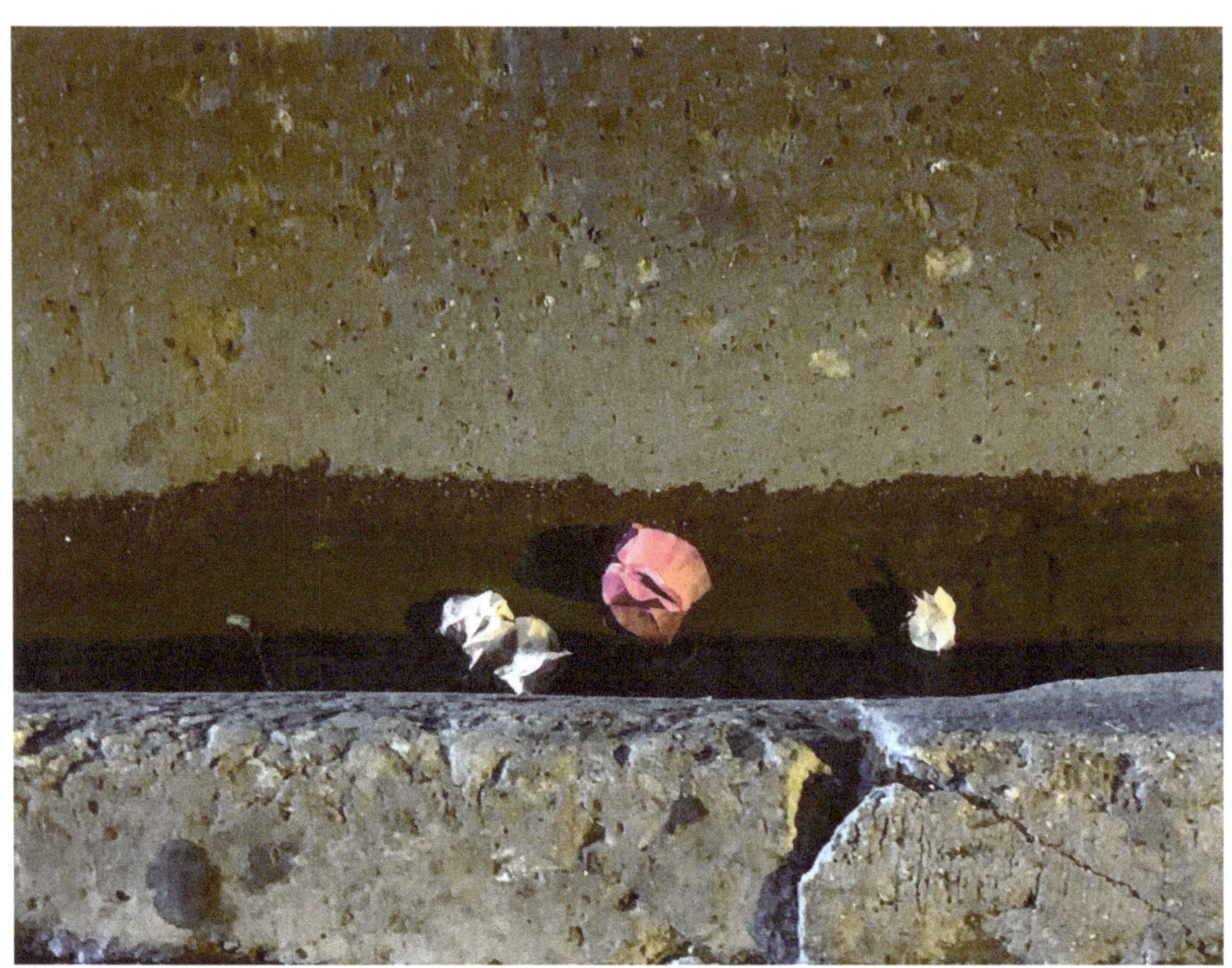

12/25

Weeks of
ambivalent anticipation
open onto
this hour.
The lit
tree's smaller.
Shiny wrappings,
Christmas tunes,
and just
we two.
My faith
abides on
a wintery
porch, joy
steeped with
melancholy, next
year trembling
under the
tree.

12/26

Christmas day's
over, but
our spirits
still want
filling. At
the art
museum, self-portraits
crowd the
walls, urging
us to consider our
alter-egos. I'm
not sure
about mine—
her guarded
eyes, hands
clutching Dad's
watch, inkpen,
flailing butterfly.

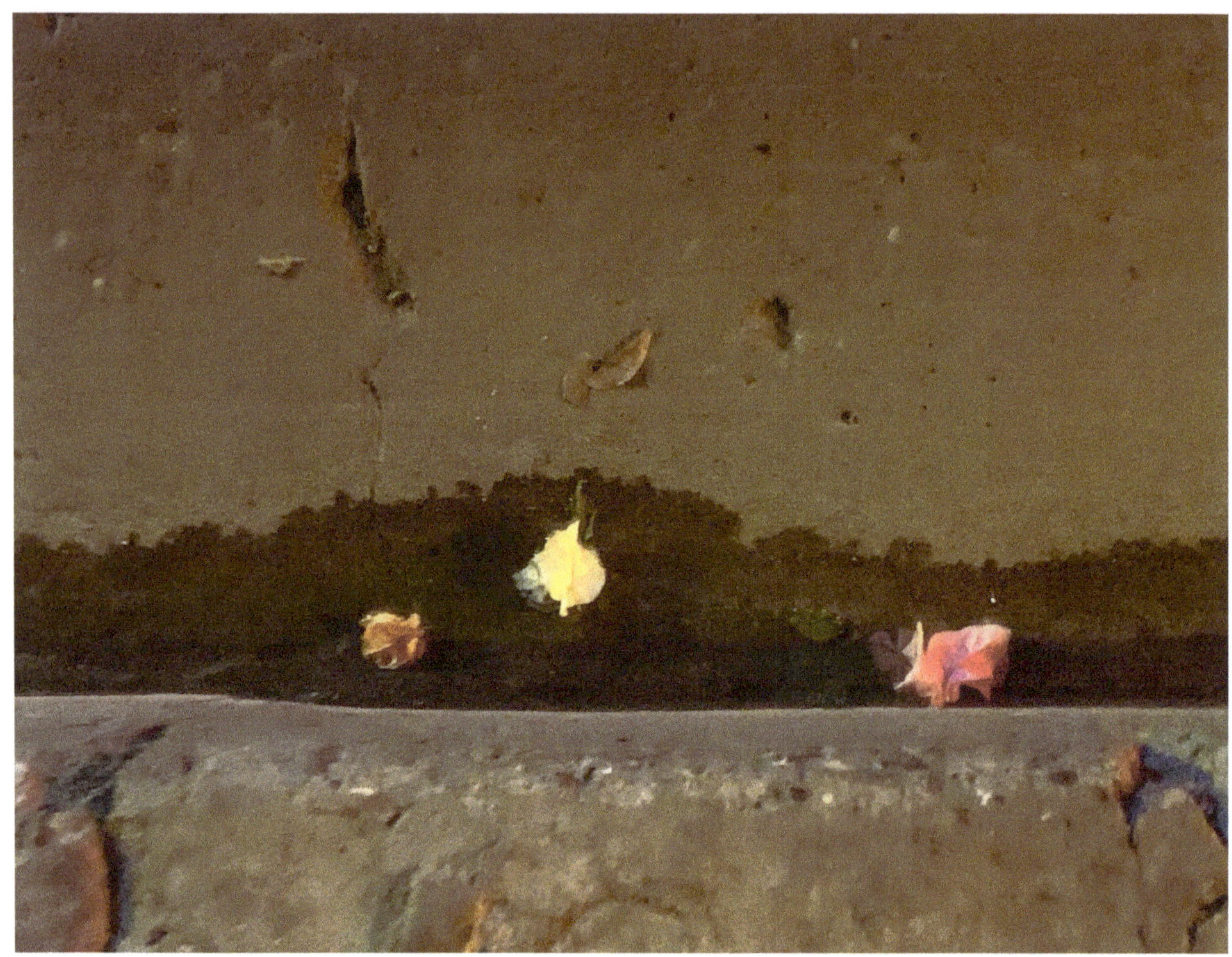

12/27

Egrets sketch
the river’s
face. We
won’t change
our ways,
despite everything,
good sense
sapped by
desire. I
reproach myself
for comings-and-goings,
turning from
flood-tides of
the dead:
330,00 faces
float across
our screens.
Egrets, leaving,
trace
their reflections.

12/28

Saying *I*
never do
this, I
shove ones
through my
half-cracked window.
He reminds
me of
my student,
tall, Black,
too clean
for thc
streets. My
son’s eyes.
He walks
on, the
light flaring
green. I
should have
given more.

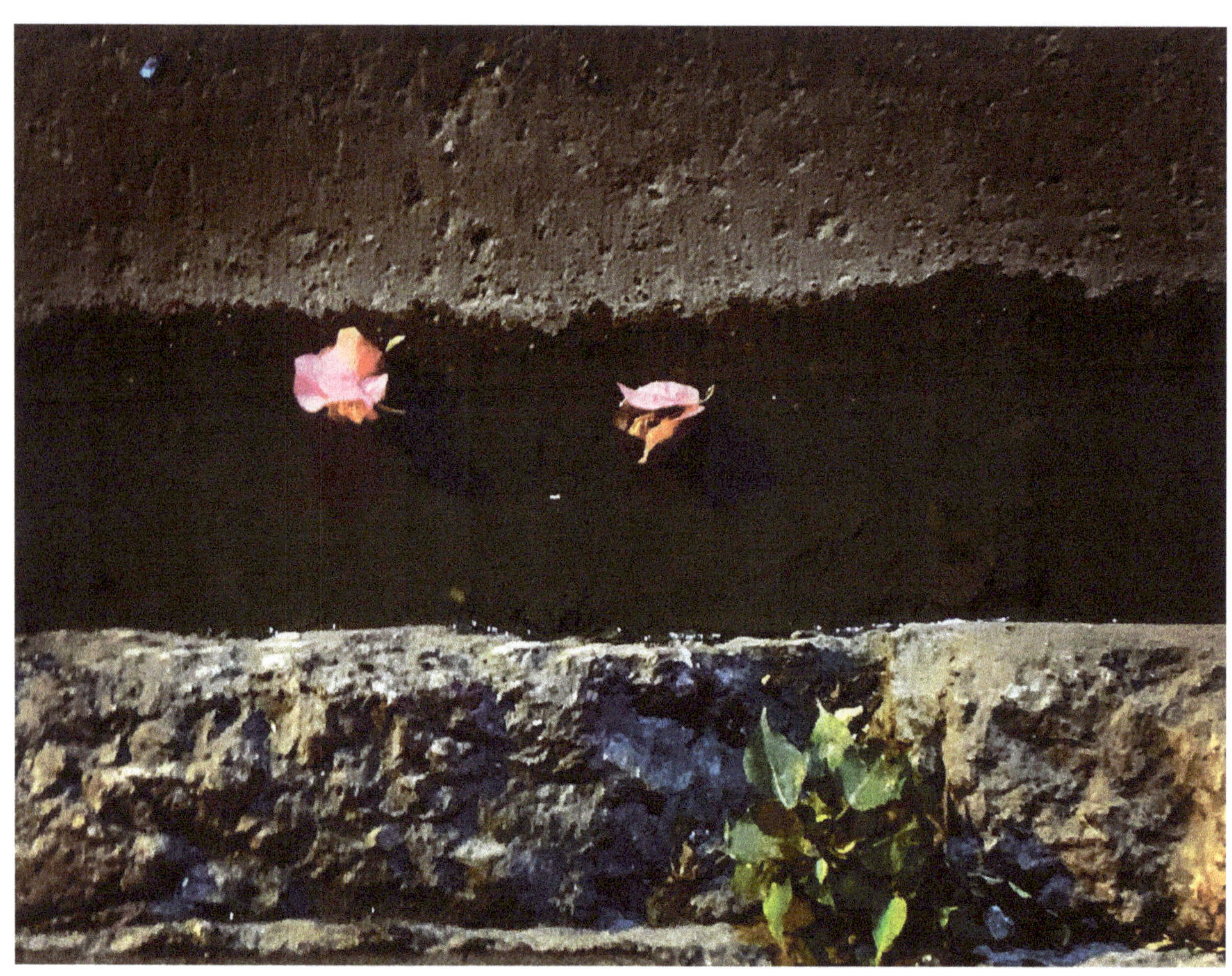

12/29

The next
to last,
next to
last night
of the year
—1 AM.
Ghost-light leaks
through half-closed
blinds. Insomnia
urges me
to the
window, dead
days falling
across the
yard. The
moon's tinted
moss and
patio silver-blue,
a gift
for my
reflection.

12/30

His cough's
a long
train of
hacking, gears
shifting in
a screech.
My weariness,
a pilled
sweater. Seems
our bodies
don't know
we're fortunate—
our home,
our work,
our big
loves.
They drag
us shaking
and cold
into tomorrow.

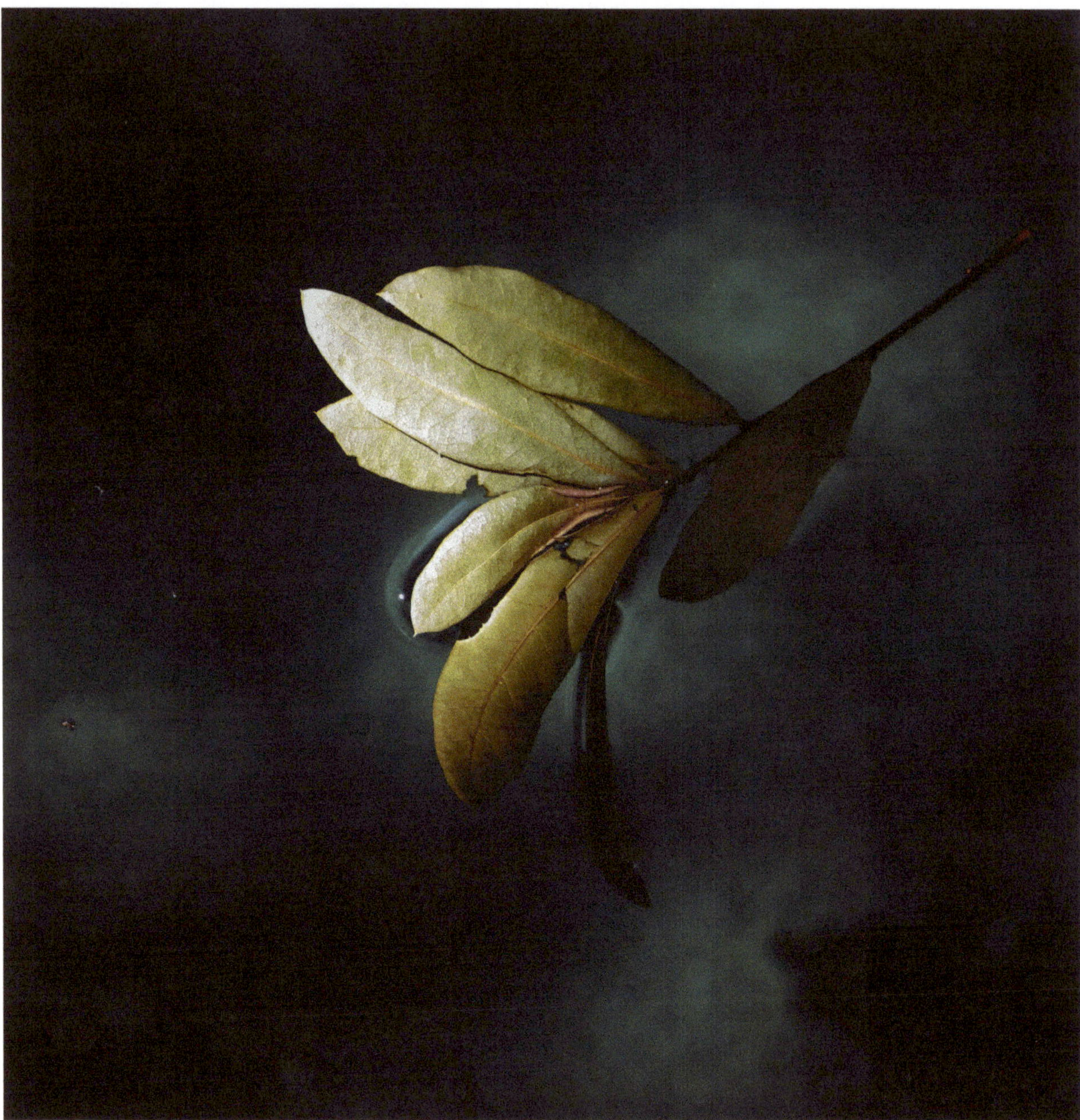

12/31 afternoon

45 minutes
I've been
here, ma'am.
He's standing
near the
Publix entrance.
I just
want food.
The deli
aisle pulses
with New
Year's Day.
Waiting, edge
of the
parking lot,
he takes
the sandwich
and chips,
yells, *Happy!*
as, embarrassed,
I lurch away.

12/31 before midnight

She's
lost her gold
bangle in
tissue-paper
waves, rivers
of wrapping paper,
an archipelago
of bows.
Gift-giving's over.
The room's
a glitter-reef
of camouflaged
disappointments,
unexpected satisfactions.
Tomorrow we'll
still be searching,
sifting through
the remains
like beachcombers
for that
small
pure
thing.

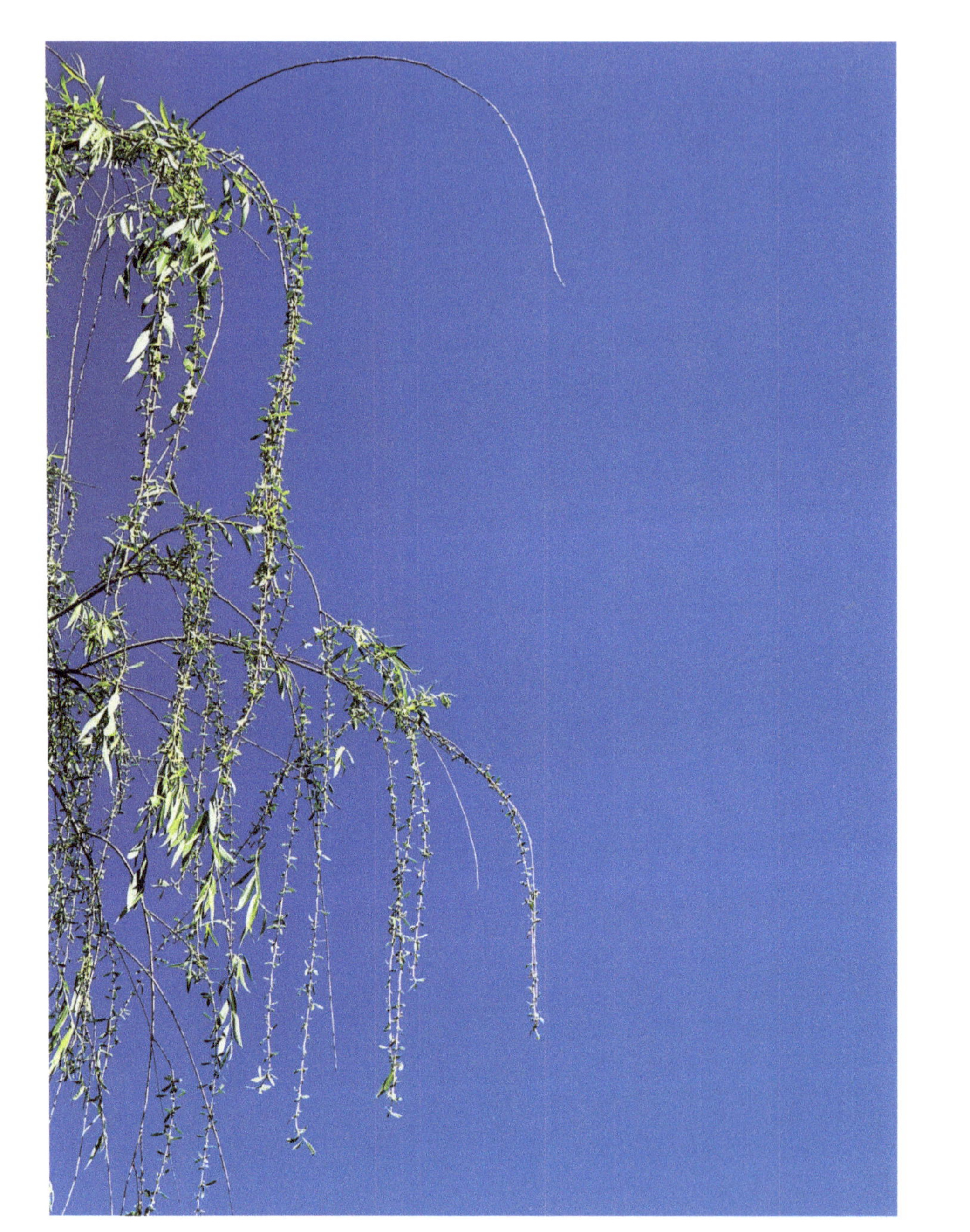

January 2021

1/1/2021

Cat's in
the window,
readying
himself for
whatever the
day may
bring. Fireworks
already unraveled
the pastel
sky. We
won't look
back. Not
forward either.
I'll serve
a tray
of delectables,
something we
can pick
up with
our fingers
like so
many wishes.

From Gianna Russo

I have many to thank for their help in bringing this project to fruition. My profound gratitude goes to the wonderful Kim Davis, poetry editor Linda Parsons, and everyone at Madville Publishing who heard these little poems singing a big song. Your support and encouragement continue to buoy me.

I am grateful to Saint Leo University for providing me with a sabbatical and the critical element of time to write these poems. Special thanks go to department chair Dr. Chantelle MacPhee; Dean, Dr. Heather Parker; and Vice President of Academic Affairs, Dr. Mary Spoto. For picking up the slack while I was on sabbatical, huge thanks and big poetry love go to my friends and colleagues Patrick Crerand, John David Harding, Angel Jimenez, and particularly Anne Barngrover, who provided thoughtful feedback on this collection, as well as enthusiastic encouragement. And of course, to Jenny, whose marvelous photos speak as eloquently as any poem.

This dailies are dedicated to my friend of forty years: poet, artist, confidante, and sister-in-spirit, Phyllis McEwen.

And to my husband, love and first reader, Jeff, whose morning coffee helped these words spring to life.

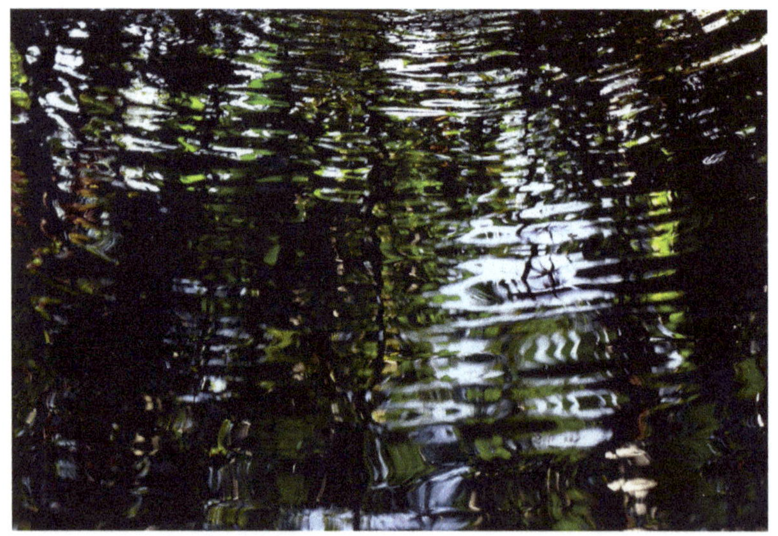

This image by Jenny called "Fairy Sighting" is dedicated to my mother, Belle Russo, who always loved fairies and their sweet magic. Do you see the fairy?

From Jenny Carey

This project was an unexpected blessing. My heartfelt gratitude to my friend and Tampa's Wordsmith, Gianna Russo. First, for her continued friendship and also for selecting my photographs to illustrate these daily poems created in 2020. Thanks also to Kim Davis of Madville Publishing, and everyone there I have yet to meet, for choosing to illustrate Gianna's poetry with photography.

My gratitude to all my friends and fellow artists of Creatives Exchange. All of them—present and past—have influenced my creative and photographic practice over the last decade. Thank you for your continued friendship and support, which I return. Special thanks to Lynn Saville, Zora Carrier, and Paul Wilborn for reviewing the project and for your support and kind words.

Thanks to Rhode Island Center for Photographic Arts in Providence, Rhode Island, and the Morean Arts Center in St. Petersburg, Florida, for including selected photographs in their exhibitions.

And to my children, Jamie and Melanie, my life would be less wonderful without you in it.

This image, a favorite of mine which we toyed with for the cover, was taken in north Georgia near the same roads Gianna traversed in 2020. If you look closely you will find a little sliver of me in the center, catching the light in the back of the photograph.

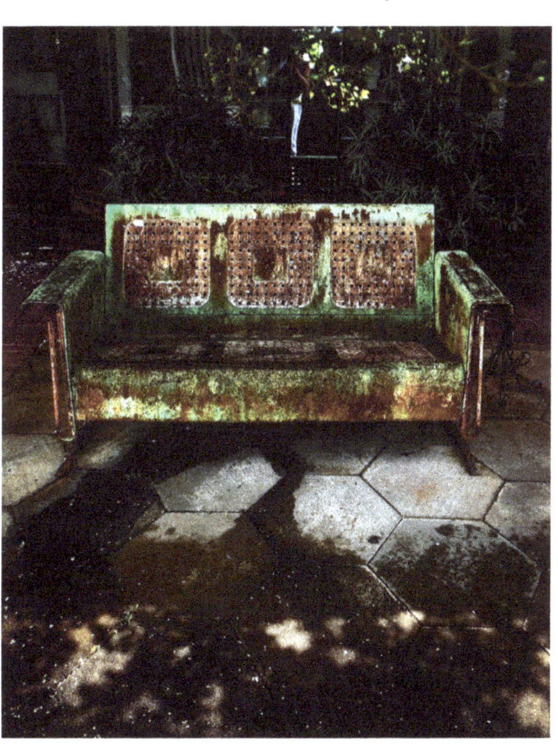

Notes on the Daily

The daily is a form that I invented in fall 2020. The form is based on a word count, determined by the month and day on which I was writing: For example, the daily word count for November 3 would be 11 (month) + 3 (day) = 14 words. I used this count for the dailies written in October, November, and December. For the January poems, I also used the number of the year for a few extra words, again adding the numerals across. For example, for January 1, 2021, I added 1 + 1 + 20 + 21 = 43.

The daily is unrhymed and includes a concrete image. In most cases, dailies have only one, two, or three words per line. With limited space, like the haiku, the daily's power is its concentration on a distinct, memorable moment that is distilled in evocative details. I believe dailies are well suited to this time of anxiety, agitation, decreased concentration, and distraction. In a few brief words, dailies illuminate the terrors and griefs and the singular beauties and joys that glint throughout our daily lives.

Notes on the poems:

10/20 ~ Early voting in Tampa

10/31 ~ Halloween

11/2 ~ Day of the Dead

11/5 ~ Mom's birthday. Belle Russo died May 19, 2009. It wasn't until I had proofed this poem several times that I realized I had accidentally written "anniversary of your death" instead of "your birth." I decided there was an inadvertent equivalency in my mistake and left it.

11/6 ~ Awaiting certification of Joe Biden as president. His presidency was certified on Nov. 7, 2020.

11/22 ~ Our 25th wedding anniversary

11/26 ~ Thanksgiving Day

11/28 ~ Our silver anniversary dinner party at home

11/29 ~ After the party

12/16 ~ First Covid vaccine given to the public

12/21 ~ Winter solstice

12/22 ~ Planetary conjunction

12/24 ~ Christmas Eve

12/25 ~ Christmas Day

12/31 ~ New Year's Eve

1/1/21 ~ New Year's Day

Notes on the Photographs

Everyday environments frame the majority of our narratives on a daily basis. These photographs in conversation with the poems are designed to create a sense of place and evoke memories of finding solace in our collective experiences of 2020. I deliberately chose to share portraits of places, intimate interiors, and natural landscapes that are open to interpretation and forgo the human figure. That absence yet a sense of presence, in the visual dialogue, illuminates shared loss. And a reminder to find joy in the everyday.

Gianna and I were not together on the same daily path during 2020, she writing poems and I photographing. Just as we all did not always walk side by side with those we loved that year. Our collaboration on *All I See Is Your Glinting* began in 2021 with the creation of a large storyboard of images. There we designed a path along the poems with photographs, like a walk through the woods or by a shore. Even in times confined inside, always finding the glinting.

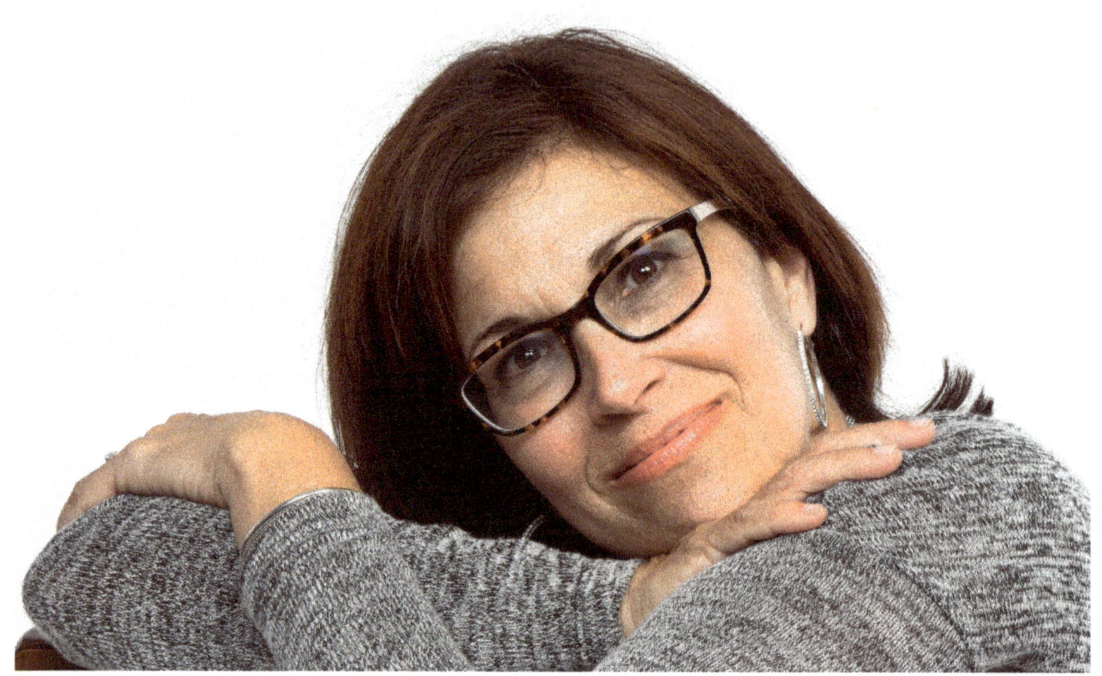

About the Poet

Gianna Russo is the inaugural Wordsmith of The City of Tampa. She is the author of the poetry collections, *One House Down* (Madville Publishing, 2019) and *Moonflower*, winner of a Florida Book Award. She has published poems in *Green Mountains Review, Gulf Stream, Negative Capability, Crab Orchard Review, Apalachee Review, The Sun, Poet Lore, saw palm, The MacGuffin, Florida Review, Tampa Review, Ekphrasis, Florida Humanities Council Forum, Karamu, The Bloomsbury Review*, and *Calyx*, among others. She is assistant professor of English and Creative Writing at Saint Leo University and serves as Saint Leo's inaugural Poet-in-Residence for the College of Arts and Sciences and scholarly journal *Rebus*. A third-generation Tampa native, a mother and grandmother, Gianna lives in an almost 100-year-old bungalow with her husband Jeff Karon and their cat Gingko.

About the Photographer

Jenny Carey is a photographic artist residing in Florida. Her work explores the themes of memory, loss, and sense of place. Ordinary subjects and intimate environments are used to evoke memories, document the intangible, and narrate unseen beauty. She began her practice as a photojournalist, and that perspective is evident in her work. Her images have been exhibited nationally, most recently at The Tampa International Airport Gallery (Florida), Manifest Gallery (Ohio), and Davis Orton (New York). Her photographic works are included in numerous private collections. The natural environment is often the subject matter in her images, but frequent travels have opened narratives with urban elements. She is the founder of Creatives Exchange, a collective of professional women artists in Tampa, Florida, where she maintains a studio practice.

www.ingramcontent.com/pod-product-compliance
Lightning Source LLC
LaVergne TN
LVHW060627110826
845147LV00015B/955